Finding the Story

PLOTTING YOUR ANCESTOR'S JOURNEY

Lynn Palermo

Lynn Palermo
12 Atwood Crescent
Simcoe On, Canada N3Y 5A4
www.familyhistorywritingstudtio.com
lynnpalermo@eastlink.ca

Cover Design by Michelina Palermo

Ordering Information:
Quantity sales. Special discounts are available on quantity purchases by genealogy and historical societies, writing groups, and others. For details, contact Lynn with subject line "Group Sales" at the email address above.

ISBN-13: 978-1519591531
ISBN-10: 1519591535

Contents

Dedicated to my ancestors who have called me to find their stories

CHAPTER 1

Why Story?

"Storytelling is the most powerful way of putting ideas into the world today."

Robert McKee

Stories are a part of our lives. We use them daily, to sell products, to convey messages, to teach and entertain. As a society, we love books, movies, television. We tell little stories every day about ourselves and each other. Stories are a powerful tool for sharing our family history research. It can be an important vehicle for delivering your family history to this generation and those to come.

Undoubtedly, as a family historian, you have boxes of family history pictures, documents, and artifacts. I know you are proud of those boxes though others may not see the value in them. I'm sure you think if they see little value in your boxes, why would they possibly embrace a book.

You've probably picked up this workbook because you have contemplated writing your family history. However, your idea of writing stories may still seem like a distant goal. You may still have objections because your family isn't interested. What is wrong with gathering your documents, pedigree charts, pictures and everything else that you have uncovered in your family history research and putting it in a box and calling it a day. You've done your part, the research, right? It's all there in the box waiting for the next generation to discover it. Hopefully, they will be interested. Why go any further and invest an immense amount of your time learning to write stories when no one is interested?

The fact that you're reading this book, I hope, indicates that you don't believe that all is lost. There exists a small light that a story, a book filled with stories could be the tool you need to break through those barriers.

Now, perhaps, you've considered assembling all your research into a nice tidy factual summary. Well, I'm sorry to disappoint you but you won't find how to do that in this book. This book is for the believers of stories. For those that believe that family history stories can, in fact, be the missing link that will bring your family closer to their history. This workbook is for those who want to write stories.

Why write stories? After all you're not a writer, you're a researcher. Why should you take the time to learn to write your family history stories? I've heard this time and again when I ask family historians if they are writing their stories. There seems a great disconnect in understanding the importance stories play in sharing our family history.

First the big box of stuff that you want to leave to the next generation is just that, stuff. It has no relevance or meaning to those who may happen to open it and look at its contents. We need to share our family history in a format that provides relevance, emotion, and meaning. Only then can readers begin to make a connection to their ancestors and their history.

As human beings, we are geared to experience the world in narrative form, which is why we love a good story. Our love of a good story is why books, movies, and television are so popular. We have a storytelling mechanism in our heads; we create millions of small narratives daily, about who we are, our experiences, fears, hopes, and relationships.

So why should family history be any different? If we want our family to take an interest, to sit up and listen, we need to format our research into a compelling story. I know it can be difficult for family historians to move from research to creative writing. However, we need to tap into the creative side of our brains and use effective techniques to tell the kind of engaging stories that will connect our families with their ancestors. Stories humanize our ancestors making it easier for our family to make a connection to them and thus their history.

Children who know their roots show higher self-esteem and a stronger sense of control over their lives. Research completed in the nineties at Emory University compared how much children knew about their families with their emotional development. Children who knew where they came from had a stronger sense of belonging to their families. They understood how their families fit into the world, and were, therefore, better able to make a connection with who they are and how they fit into their environment. Family history stories are significant to our children's development and our association to each other and our world.

It isn't just necessary to write a narrative, but we are obliged to write entertaining stories to draw our readers in so we can deliver the educational and inspiring components of our history that engage our family and descendants.

Stories are used to entertain, certainly, but they also have the ability to educate, inspire and motivate and if you are lucky they can do all of these. However, the only way you can teach your readers about their family history, the only way you can inspire them and motivate them to understand more of their family history, and perhaps even take up the torch of becoming the keeper of the family history sto-

2

ries is first to entertain. Amuse them first, with a story that is full of colour and well-defined ancestors, with action, and settings that jump off the page. You want to bring them on a journey, give them an ancestor to root for, an ancestor in which they can connect with emotionally.

Once we tell a great story that gives our reader that emotional connection to their ancestor they will by association make that same connection to their history. They will begin to question what other wonders hide in their family history. You can write stories that influence a generation, provide stories they will carry with them and influence how they forever look at the world and their purpose in it.

Our goal in this workbook is to help you find your family history story. This workbook is going to help you do just that in three very specific ways. First, this book will offer you are a variety of choices for looking at your ancestors and your research to help you *find the story you want to tell*. This workbook isn't about reciting a cradle-to-grave account of a person's life. It is about looking for an achievement, a goal, a desire in your ancestor's life, perhaps even a teaching moment through which to tell your family history. Secondly, we are going to help you *find the events in your ancestor's story that align with the parts of a story.* Being able to understand the parts of a story and identify them in your research as a part of your ancestor's legend is a significant step to telling a story. Thirdly, we will help *you find the structure of your story and map it, so you have a guide for your writing*. Our story map will be an instrumental tool in outlining your story. We will give you the tools to write a story full of action and suspense, a story that goes beyond the physical exploits of your ancestor's story. It will help you layer action, theme, and the inner journey for your readers.

This workbook will not write the story for you. However, it will give you the direction, the structure, and the tools you need to find your story and your way to an entertaining, educational and inspirational family history narrative.

A great story will transport your readers to another place and time, a time when their ancestors walked. A time when they made decisions, sacrifices and battled inner demons to make better lives for themselves, their families and their descendants. A great story will bring your ancestor to life, let us peek inside their homes, their work, their lives, it will allow us to walk beside them, watch events unfold as if we are guests in their homes. This is the power you hold as a family history writer. Now let's tap into that power.

Let's find the stories you want to write.

CHAPTER 2

Finding Story Ideas

"The more you know about, the more likely you are to combine

things to make an idea that's striking."

James Patterson

You can take several approaches when it comes to looking at your ancestors, their lives, and your research to identify the story you want to tell. Some of you may already know the story you wish to tell while others may have no idea. You may have many ancestors in your research to choose from. It's not necessary to tell a story about every ancestor in your family history. What is crucial is to find the stories that are the perfect conduit for delivering your research and your history.

Don't fear to embrace a variety of approaches. It can sometimes not only help you find a story but find a better story. By better, I mean a more captivating story that can keep your readers committed to the end. The key here is to have an open mind to all the possibilities. Sometimes the most obvious is not necessarily the best choice. Of course, writers choose a story based on their views and biases of their ancestor and their family history. My goal is not to persuade you to change your mind, but only help you look beyond the most obvious option and to offer you choices.

CAUSE AND EFFECT

A story is built on scenes with a dependence on each other. Cause and effect in and between scenes allow you to lead the reader to each major event seamlessly by linking the cause in one scene to the result in the next scene; it's like a chain. This sequencing allows the story to rise in action smoothly. If the scenes fall out of sequence or scenes come out of the blue, the chain weekends and becomes disconnected. As you begin to look at story ideas, it's important to keep in mind the idea of cause and effect as you look for your story and how the events in your ancestor's life depend on each other.

FAMILY HISTORY RESEARCH

The first and obvious place to look for your story is in your research. Look for those fascinating and unusual situations that occurred in your ancestor's life. You know the saying "truth is stranger than fiction," often it is very true. You may find some information in your research that is just a great story because it is unique and different with a dramatic conflict with stakes and emotion attached to it. Often a single document, picture, event, or artifact can propel such a story.

CONFLICTS AND COMPLICATIONS

Conflict is a crucial part of a story. No conflict, no story. Therefore, the best place to find a story is in the conflict in your ancestor's life. Look for those difficult times that challenged your ancestor. Conflict can come in a variety of shapes.

Consider the following:

Human vs. Human
Human vs. Nature
Human vs. Self
Human vs. Technology
Human vs. Fate/Destiny/God
Human vs. Society

THE END RESULT

While the conflict might be the easiest and most obvious place to begin, I always suggest considering accomplishments, solutions, knowledge or an answer that your ancestor achieved in his life. If your ancestor has achieved success, for instance, became a doctor, immigrated to the New World, obtained freedom from slavery, or became a landowner, there is often a degree of challenge that your ancestor had to overcome to attain this result. It there wasn't any challenge it couldn't have been much of an accomplishment. Look for an accomplishment along with the challenges and conflicts faced to achieve that goal and you've likely found yourself a good story.

Here are some results to consider:

Problem — Solution
Mystery — Solution

Conflict — Peace
Danger — Safety
Confusion — Order
Dilemma — Decision
Ignorance — Knowledge
Question — Answer

ASK WHY AND WHAT IF?

Family historians who find great stories look past the facts on the page. They plow beneath the surface; they ask the important question. Why? They imagine their ancestors, how would they behave in such a circumstance. When we conduct our family history research, we acquire the who, when and where. However, often we don't ask why. Why did our ancestor immigrate? Why did they sell their house? Why did they migrate to the country? Why did they leave their family? It is in the why that the story lives. The why often reveals the stakes and the motivations for their decisions and these stakes and motivations are an important ingredient in our stories.

LOOK FOR A COMPLEX HERO

Every good story has a fascinating character behind it. I would encourage you to look for the everyday heroes in your family history. Now, be careful these aren't superheroes. An everyday hero is someone who has done something that appears quite regular and mundane to most, but in retrospect their decision has made a remarkable difference in the lives of others. Everyday heroes are complex with both faults and strengths and by virtue they allow the reader to embrace them and root for them. Find these ancestors, they are often disguised as the common man but, in fact, are a hero to their families.

START WITH YOURSELF

Finding story ideas can often grow from your interests, ideas, biases, and prejudices. I hear your objection already. "I don't want this to be about me. I want to write an unbias tale of my ancestor's history."

An unbias story does not exist, there is no such thing. Every decision you make about the story you write filters through your interests, biases, and prejudices. There is no getting away from it nor should you. Ask yourself, what ancestors are you drawn to and why? Is there something you can or can't identify with in their life? Is there a decision they made that you would have done differently? If you are intrigued by a particular ancestor or an event or a decision your ancestor made in their life chances are other members of your family are going to be intrigued as well. Remember, you are the writer, you must be passionate about your topic. Sure you're fanatical about family history, but drill down further what or who specifically within your family history captures your attention.

What you believe in is who you are, and determines how you view the world and therefore how you observe your family history and therefore how you will shape and write a story. Your point of view will determine your approach to telling a family history story.

Here's a simple exercise. Write ten things to describe yourself.

For instance, I would describe myself as a:

1. Mother
2. Wife
3. Writer
4. Spiritual
5. Friend
6. Coach
7. Creative
8. Student
9. Sister
10. Volunteer

Try this out for yourself. As you explore each of these titles you have given yourself, consider connecting your ideas about yourself with those of your ancestors. Perhaps you share several identities with an ancestor; perhaps you are on opposite ends with an ancestor. Each may pose an opportunity for a story. Our stories lie with our ancestor's relationship to their world, to others around them, as well as to the writer and, therefore, the reader.

GET TO KNOW YOUR ANCESTOR

How would your ancestor answer the above question? What ten titles would they choose to describe themselves? If you've done your homework in workbook number two, Authentic Ancestors, then most likely you can answer this question. Authentic Ancestors was all about helping you develop a deep understanding of your ancestor. Hopefully through the Authentic Ancestor Profile you would be able to see past both your ancestor's exterior makeup but also get inside their head. Undoubtedly, by now, you can think a little more deeply about your ancestor, who they were and why they made the choices they made in their lives.

ARTIFACTS LEFT BEHIND

Diaries, letters, artifacts, and photographs are places to seek out stories. Artifacts left by ancestors can be a great place to look for a story, whether the story lies in the relationship between the artifact and the ancestor or the journey of the artifact. Is the item a symbol or theme for your ancestor's life. For example, a trunk full of letters, while the letters will hold significant information, the fact that your ancestor kept the trunk full of letters says something about her as well. Why do some ancestors keep these notes while others do not? The fact that you are keeping the correspondences, what does that say about you, how does that connect you to your ancestor? Look for connections between your ancestor, yourself and your reader, they may surprise you what stories they hold.

THE SUBJECT IS ALWAYS A QUESTION

Subjects of stories often lie with the question. Consider the following:

What is it like to be a cowboy in Texas in the 1800's?
What is it like to be a midwife in Northern Canada?
What's it like to be a farmer in Midwest America?

Look at your ancestor and ask yourself a question about their life. Now try to answer it, this is your story.

COLLABORATION

Sit down with some family or even friends and tell them some stories within your family history research. Which story intrigues them the most? What questions do they have about the story or their family history? These can often be great places to find a story idea. Why should we consider friends as well as family? If you can intrigue people outside your family circle with a family history story, chances are it's a pretty good story and worth your time and energy.

WORLD, REGIONAL AND LOCAL RESEARCH

Learn about the world and the events that took place around your ancestor and during your ancestor's time on this earth. The more you know about the world around your ancestor, the more story ideas you may begin to see. You begin to see the influences the world played in your ancestor's stories and these pressures may have increased the stakes considerably for your ancestor, proving a much more engaging story than you initially might have thought.

TRY A DIFFERENT VIEW

We often gravitate toward a particular ancestor when considering a story. Taking a different view could lead you to an entirely dissimilar and amazing story. Look at your story from the viewpoint of a different ancestor. Maybe you planned to write a story from your great-grandfather's perspective but it's not working out. Perhaps the story is better told from his son's perception or his wife's angle. There are many views of a family history. If you're not finding the story at the current angle, try changing views.

LOOK AT THE WORLD AROUND YOU

Sometimes I can be walking down the street, and something happens that leads me to wonder about how a situation may have happened in my ancestor's day. How did they face a particular problem? How did they overcome an obstacle I face today. Sometimes triggers in our life can open up some story ideas to investigate in your ancestor's life.

LOOK FOR EMOTION

If you find yourself touched about a particular story chances are others will as well. It's important for your readers to make an emotional bond to their ancestor. Looking for a story with a particularly strong emotional element is a great place to start. Do you have a strong reaction to a story? Trust your instincts, most likely others will as well.

CAPTURE YOUR STORY IDEAS

Devise a plan to record your story ideas. You may be deep in the throes of research and not ready to write, or you just may be going about your day when an idea occurs to you. Make sure you put in place a system to record your story ideas. You can keep a story file, or a notebook, or a recipe box with index cards recording an idea on each card. You can go digital and keep your notes on your computer or your cell phone. Find a way to jot down the ideas whenever and wherever they strike you. But don't just got them down, keep track of them, file them, catalogue them for later use.

Some of these ideas may not pan out and may never make the page, but keeping track of them for later review is a vital step in finding the stories. Don't leave your story ideas up to your memory. We are bombarded daily with information, and it can be hard to recall an idea later when we are ready to use it. Put a plan in place to record your ideas so you can easily review them when you are read

CHAPTER 3

The Story Recipe

"Story is a yearning meeting an obstacle."

Robert Olen Butler

To write a family history narrative, you first must understand the ingredients of a story. According to two-time Pulitzer Prize winner and master of the nonfiction short story, Jon Franklin,

"a story consists of a sequence of actions that occur when a sympathetic character encounters a complicating situation that he confronts and solves."

I like to think of a story as a recipe for a favourite dish. All stories have a common set of attributes, ingredients that come together to produce something scrumptious. You are the chef, who must learn your craft as there is no magic, it takes time and practice. Your first task is to find those ingredients. You must pick them from your research like a mother harvesting from her garden. You then bring them together, in just the right amounts, with love and care, to create a beautiful dish your family will love.

Without these particular ingredients, the story will not take shape. When something is missing from the recipe the taste of our dish falls flat; it lacks luster. It's important to have all the ingredients in the story in just the right amounts to make the dish shine, the same goes for your story.

The ingredients in our story plot recipe include:

Character
Conflict
Setting
Theme
Resolution

STORY INGREDIENT NO. 1

CHARACTER

Every story starts with a character, in our case an ancestor. Our ancestors are the soul of the story. Our stories revolve around them.

Every story must have a protagonist from which we can focus the story. By identifying this protagonist ancestor, your readers will see their family history through their eyes. The reader will make an emotional connection with the ancestor, and that is what we want. Once the reader has made that connection they will be hooked. They will want to know more.

We look for three qualities in our ancestor.

Every major character in a story has a goal that is ultimately the heart of the story. In a story, a reader stays to see if the main character reaches their goal. Your ancestor's goal is motivated by something in their life, usually in their history, an experience, or an event that may have had a substantial impact on them and their actions. Also, if they don't achieve their goal, they fear a loss. It could be an apparent loss as in a material item, money or land, or even the loss of life, or it could be internal losses, such as respect or honour.

Before you begin to write your story, it's important to recognize the goals, motivations, and stakes of your ancestor. They are critical not only understanding your ancestor but also in shaping their story.

GOAL

WHAT DOES YOUR ANCESTOR WANT?

As humans we seek many different materials and or emotional wants; these are our goals. Your family history story needs a goal, which means your Protagonist Ancestor needs a goal. Where do I find the objective of my ancestor? Look at the actions in their lives. Look at the events on their timeline, did they emigrate, why? Did they own land, did they fight in a war, did they become famous, or influential in politics, did they have a large family? Our ancestor's actions are clues to what they valued in life, their goals, the wants or desires that they valued most in life.

Does your ancestor want something so badly that they are prepared to destroy or be destroyed to attain this goal?

To make sacrifices?

To take risks?

Did they join the army because they believe in the cause?

Did they leave the country because they didn't support the cause?

Of course, not all goals are created equally, the bigger the goal, the more exciting the story, the more moving the story, the more gripping the read. Try to find a goal that you feel will provide a big story and will connect with your family. Stop thinking of your family history as a chronological timeline of events, rather a desire with obstacles to overcome on the path to it.

Your ancestor's goal could be a physical goal such as to own land, or to gain his freedom. Or perhaps his goal is emotional, to gain confidence, to earn the respect of his fellow man. Or perhaps acquiring a material object will affect your ancestor's emotional state. We will talk more about his emotional journey a little later. For now understand that the internal goal, or what we will call the ***inner journey*** is the emotional arc of your story, and to make your story truly powerful it's important to see how your ancestor changed as he moved closer to achieving his accomplishments.

MOTIVATION

WHY DOES YOUR ANCESTOR WANT IT?

Once you've determined the goal of your story, the next step is to understand your ancestor's motivation. Why did your ancestor have this particular goal? Each human being who walked this Earth had wants and desires that were driven by a motivation. Through your research, you want to come to understand what that motivation may be. For example, if your ancestor's goal was to own land, what in their history, their past motivated that desire? Look at motivation as the backstory to the need.

STAKES

WHAT WILL HAPPEN? WHAT COULD HAPPEN IF YOUR ANCESTOR HAD FAILED TO MEET HIS GOALS?

The stakes are why we keep reading, if there is nothing at stake, no risk, there is little reason to keep turning the page. Of course, not all stories are life-or-death stakes. Again big stakes produce powerful stories. While the risks may not necessarily be life or death, our ancestors faced some very real stakes. For example, war, poverty, deportation, inscription, jail, poorhouses are only a few of the outcomes that may have occurred if they had not taken actions towards their goals. Whether your ancestor failed and succumbed to the stakes, or were driven by stakes to succeed, the point is the stakes, raise the risk. Therefore, the more risk, the more tension, and the more tension, the more likely your reader stays engaged.

The goals, motivations, and stakes of your ancestor are the heart of your story, along with the elements on which to shape your family history story plot.

I believe it is possible for a family historian to bring their ancestors to live on the page, give them a face, emotions and motivations all while drawing from research, facts, and social history. Characterization is the tool we use in creative nonfiction to make this happen. Characterization gives us the opportunity to make our ancestors vivid for our readers through details, description, dialogue and a complete understanding of their lives before and after the scope of the story.

When we write a family history, some of the work of characterization is done for us. Our ancestor lived. The family history is a matter of fact. The physical description defined for us. Our ancestor's actions played out. You think that would make it easier. However, unlike fiction, our job does not fall into making things up but in doing justice to the facts, filtering our research through our emotions, biases, and experiences. We must dig deep to understand our ancestor and make them dance on the page. We must have an intimate understanding of who they were on a variety of levels.

Our job is to engage our readers by connecting them with our ancestors, characters in the story. Characters drive stories, not events. Your reader does not invest in a narrative because of an event. While it helps to structure your story around events, readers invest in a book because they make an emotional connection with the character. They root for them; something about them resonates with them, and they want to know what happens to them. We want the same to hold for our family history stories. We want our readers to love our ancestors and to find an emotional bond to them. When we achieve this, not only will they fall in love with the story, but they will have a stronger desire to know more about their family history. After all, this is our ultimate goal, to have our family see the reward in realizing their history. This realization is why we need characterization when we write our family history stories.

In our family history, we look to a variety of sources to draw out our ancestor's character.

A physical description
Their possessions
Their dialogue
Their actions and reactions
Their written words
Anecdotes
What others say and write about them
Other's reactions to them

14

Character profiles or in the case of family history, an ancestor profile is an ideal tool to capture the information needed to paint this picture. A character profile assists the writer in realizing a character that is life like and it helps the writer make sure there is a continuity throughout the story. An ancestor profile helps you organize your thoughts about an individual ancestor, keep track of their idiosyncrasies and relationships. It can help you flesh out an ancestor that you've never met, and fully realize the physical, physiological and sociological makeup of your ancestor.

You will find an extensive Ancestor Profile worksheet in Workbook 2, Authentic Ancestors, with instructions for completing it.

I encourage you if you have not already done so to work your way through Workbook 2 and complete an Authentic Ancestor Profile. You will be far better prepared to use the information to structure your plot in this workbook and to write your scenes that will speak to not only the dramatic action, the outer story, but the inner story as well.

STORY INGREDIENT NO. 2

CONFLICT

A story does not exist without conflict. You're probably thinking at this point, well, my ancestors weren't chased by bad guys, they didn't fight to save the world, there is no conflict in their life and, therefore, no story to tell. They were farmers and peasants who lived rather mundane lives. As human beings we face struggles, tension, complications in our lives, our ancestors were no different. If you haven't found the conflict, the struggle in your ancestor's life than I suspect you haven't looked hard enough. You haven't gone below the surface. This tension is the difference between the way things are and the way our ancestors would like them to be. This is tension in your story and without identifying that tension, it's unlikely your readers will be interested.

One of the fundamental components of any good family history story is recognizing a conflict your ancestor faced in their life and bringing that to the front of the story. We discussed in chapter three that looking for conflict is one way to find your story in your research.

Conflict creates a story question. How does my ancestor overcome this conflict, this challenge? The reader wants the answer and, for this reason, stays with the story to the end, to get the question answered.

By the end of the beginning of your story, you want your readers to understand your ancestor's challenge and how they intend to overcome this problem. We will talk more about the beginning, middle, and end a little later. However, remember that the story question comes in the first quarter of your story, setting up your reader to follow you.

Let's create an ancestor, Henry Jones, for demonstrating conflict and obstacles, and follow him through a story plot. Of course, in your family history, your going to pull this information from your research.

We start by understanding Henry's goal.

Henry's Goal: Henry Jones wants to own land. Of course, for this to be a story there must be some conflict, some challenge in Henry's pursuit of that goal.

Henry's Conflict– Henry cannot own land in his current country, the land is owned by the wealthy. Henry is a peasant and will spend his life farming the land of the rich.

The First Turning Plot Point – This is the moment when your ancestor makes a decision that changes his path in pursuit of his goal. This is also often called the inciting incident. Henry makes the decision to emigrate to the New World, where land is plentiful.

Obstacles

In our family history story, obstacles block our ancestor on their path to achieving their goals. In a story plot, they are often referred to as plot points.

There are three types of obstacles that your ancestor may confront:

ancestor vs. another person

ancestor vs. circumstance

ancestor vs. self

WHAT IS THE DIFFERENCE BETWEEN CONFLICT AND OBSTACLE?

The conflict is the overall idea; Henry cannot own land. The obstacles are those roadblocks that stand between Henry resolving his desire to own land.

Keep in mind that both conflicts and obstacles may be both internal and external, they can come from within the protagonist or from external forces, friendly and not so friendly.

If we continue to follow the example above, our ancestor Henry who wished to own land may come up against many obstacles.

Henry's Obstacles

Obstacle 1 – Henry arrives in the United States, there is plenty of land but he must head west, Henry has no money to get there. He overcomes this obstacle by getting a job. (**ancestor vs. circumstance**)

Obstacle 2 – He's saving his money and close to leaving when he meets the love of his life. But, Mary doesn't want to leave her family behind and travel west for land; Henry must convince her this decision is in their best interest. (**ancestor vs. another person**)

Obstacle 3 – Along the way they fall on hardships, and Henry doubts his choices. (**ancestor vs. self**)

Obstacle 4 – A violent storm delays their journey. (**ancestor vs. circumstance**)

The obstacles tell a story, but also show growth of your ancestor, from poor to rich, sad to happy, hate to love, weak to strong.

Look at your research, what obstacles did your ancestor face in pursuit of his goals?

STORY INGREDIENT NO. 3

SETTING

An important part of writing our ancestor's stories is building the world where they lived. Crafting a genuine world is a key to transporting our readers back in time. It's not enough to just state the year and the location of your story, you have to show your reader how that world looks. You can't assume your reader will know anything about the period your ancestor lived. They need the writer, you, to build the world, paint the picture, give colour, texture, and emotion to that world so that it comes to life for them and they are transported back in time.

Writers build the world on the page through detail and description, and you'll do the same as a family history writer. The world that emerges from the page will allow the reader not just to read about it but travel back in time and experience it.

UNDERSTAND THE HISTORY OF THE TIME

It's important to understand world history, the politics, economics and social conventions of the time. Who was in power at the time? Why? What was the major trade? Marriage laws? To write about a particular time, you must become very familiar with the time. Researching the period, and all matters related to that time is tremendously important to establishing that world. By referring to the history of the time, perhaps even referring to historical figures you help your reader connect with the time and place.

KNOW THE LOCAL COMMUNITY

It's not enough to know what was happening in the world, you must have a strong sense of what was occurring locally, and understanding the makeup of the community where your ancestor lived. Did they live in a city or a small town? What was the topography of the area? Was the landscape hilly or flat? What was the weather like? Did they experience the four seasons? Was the community in close proximity or distant? Who were their neighbours? What was happening in the local politics? Were your ancestor's well known in the community or outsiders?

HOW WERE THEY AFFECTED?

Once we identify the historical world, regional and local events relevant your ancestor's timeline we have to interpret how those events may have affected your ancestor. Is there any correlation between those events and your ancestor's actions? Don't just lay on historical information into your story. Weave the historical data into the events and actions of your ancestor's life as seen through the lens of your ancestor. How does he or she feel about particular events? Don't know how they felt, perhaps their actions reveal their attitudes?

SENSE IT.

Use your five senses when building your ancestor's world. Your senses are an important part of bringing the surroundings to your readers. The sight of land as the ship arrives at its port, the smell of the city, the music playing, the sound of the cars or horses coming down the road, the touch of a wedding dress. The use of your senses makes the surroundings come alive for your reader.

DRESS IT.

 Make sure you know what your ancestor is wearing, what undergarments support it, what was considered appropriate or risqué, and what kind of dress would suit your ancestor based on their station in life, their occupation, their religion and their attitudes. You may not necessarily have a picture of your ancestor, but dress and grooming of the time can help you piece together an image of your ancestor for your reader.

DETAIL IT.

Details bring the world to life. The more intimate the detail, the more your reader can envision that world. It's important just not to list details and to lay it on thick but to choose those particulars wisely. Instead, look for details that you can weave into the story. What clothes they wore, the food on their plate, the book they were reading. Other details that add authenticity to your narrative include transportation, furniture, medicine, language, etc. We need to go under the surface of the story; to know what life was like in that era and how your ancestor experienced that world.

Writing the physical world of our ancestors may seem impossible at times. We face two concerns, how do we know what it looked like and how do we bring that world to the page.

Replicating that world will rely heavily on your family history research and social history research. I encourage you, where possible to visit the ancestral hometowns of your ancestors. Walk the streets, visit the local historical societies and learn everything you can about their surroundings, from the house they lived in, to the street they lived on. Absorb the town that was a part of their daily life. If you can't go in person, visit through the magic of Google Earth. Reproduce your ancestor's setting to the most intimate detail.

A setting can also establish mood and tone, and it can be a character in of itself. For example, the supportive small town or the thick forest holding back progress or a chaotic city that overwhelms a new resident can play a pivotal role in a story. The setting can offer far more complications or support in your story than just a pretty backdrop in which to tell your story. What you choose to share in terms of details are the very tools you will use to create tone and evoke feeling. Is the kitchen warm and cozy, or cold and desolate? The description you share should be hand-picked and carefully worded to evoke the feelings you want to bring forward to the reader.

The setting can also take on a character type role. Many of you writing memoir might find this true when writing about a childhood home, or a grandparent's house, a setting that conjures great emotion.

STORY INGREDIENT NO. 4

THEME

How you tell your story depends on what is important to you.

How you write it, the message you wish it to leave with your reader is your individual decision as the author of your family history story. How you frame this story compared to how I would frame the same story is what sets us apart. It's what you as the writer; the artist brings to the story and the page.

As you begin to develop your family history story plot, get to know your ancestors as characters. Consider plotting their conflict and obstacles on a story map so that you will start to see beyond just the structure of your story. You acquire some ideas, thoughts and messages that will help you develop your story and offer a deeper meaning for your reader.

While it's important to understand the story question, and the theme behind your story it's also important to comprehend why you are writing this story. Why are you willing to take time away from another area of your life to develop this story? What is it you want to say and why? Where is this story coming from inside you? If you understand the answers to those questions not only will you have a stronger story, you'll find the discipline to stay focused and complete your story.

Keep revisiting and refining the theme until you know the point, the message you are trying to make. You may not recognize this right away, but as you write your draft and even through your revisions you'll begin to see the message of your family history story. We will talk more about how to do this in later chapters.

The story question you choose to spotlight in your tale and, subsequently, answer, is again one of those unique choices you get to make as the author. Consider the story question you have chosen and why you have chosen it to help you uncover the themes in your story.

Your story motivation is not to be confused with your ancestor's motivation. Rather consider what is motivating you, the author, to write this story. Where is your story coming from? Consider why this story is important to you? What are you trying to say? Why did you choose this particular ancestor, this particular story? What is your motivation to tell this story? Why does it resonate with you? By taking a few minutes to address your motivation, it will help you to peel back the layers of your story and help you to find the theme. By considering theme, the story question, and the motivations behind your decisions and subsequently their relationship to one another, you place yourself on the path to developing a stronger, in-depth and resonating story for your readers. You not only build a story, but you deliver a message to your audience that will stay long after the last page.

STORY INGREDIENT NO. 5

RESOLUTION

All stories have an ending, a resolution. Your character ends at a different place from where he began. Of course, not all stories have a happy ending, but by the end of the story your character has grown, changed or learned something new, and without this change, you don't have much of a story.

In writing stories about our ancestors, we aren't necessarily provided with nice tidy endings in which all problems are solved. Of course, you cannot create happy endings to satisfy your reader. When it comes to writing our ancestors stories your story should end somewhere different from where it began. By the end of your story, your ancestor or yourself, if it is a memoir, should have changed or grown or learned something new. Without this change, you don't have a story.

Characters, conflicts, plots, settings, theme, and resolutions, these are the ingredients that a great family history story. By combining these elements and crafting them into a structure, you will be able to tell your tale in a compelling, entertaining, and fulfilling way.

CHAPTER 4

Universal Story

"The art exists purely in the arrangement of words."

Philip Gerrard

All stories at their core follow the same blueprint. The story begins, it expands, it contracts and closes. This pattern is true of all stories despite their genre. No matter whether you are reading a romance or comedy, a horror or crime story, science-fiction or historical fiction, memoirs and yes, even family history narrative, this pattern stands firm.

The Universal Story from it's earliest time remains steadfast today. As a family history writer, you tap into and use this tool structure and tell your stories, you'll provide your readers with the ability to connect with their ancestors and their history on a deeper and more profound level.

Many family history writers just jump into writing and give little thought to the structure of their story. They start thinking about their ancestors and restrict their story to a chronological format; you know that overused birth to death arrangement. They begin writing at what they believe is the beginning of the story with little thought to the journey the reader is going to take and whether that voyage will hold the reader's attention. They start thinking about sentences and words, more of the polish that comes at the end. Thinking about sentences and words is like thinking about paint and wallpaper when you're building a house when you don't even have a blueprint or walls. The plot structure is your blueprint to your family history story. It will be your visual guide to assembling your story. Taking the time upfront to determine the structure of your story will help you immensely in creating that fascinating read for your family. Taking the time to plot your story on a narrative arc of the classic universal storyline can help you frame your ancestor's internal and external journey.

A family history story transports your reader to your ancestor's world via experience. Not through arguments or facts but through the illusion that his life is taking place on the page. I believe, that it is not the facts, the research that will convince your family to take an interest in their history but the story. The power of story, and more specifically, the use of a plot structure that will help you frame your story and obtain that goal.

Every plot has the same structure, a narrative arc. In a basic narrative for a nonfiction family history, an ancestor pursues a goal. He faces a series of conflicts and obstacles and as a result, his choices, his ideas, and thoughts change over time. In the end, the ancestor is transformed, and his transformation creates a different understanding of his existence.

The plot is not just a sequence of events showing dramatic action. In addition to that dramatic action we also want to see an emotional change in our ancestor, as well as a theme, a teaching moment we want our readers to grasp.

To avoid telling your family tale in a this happened, and then that happened and then something else happened fashion, you must enlist plot. The plot is a series of events related causally. This happened because that other thing happened. Of course, because we are writing nonfiction we can't make things up. We can't say this happened because of this if that's not the case. However, we can be artful in how to demonstrate coherence and meaning through how you arrange the parts of your story.

You can't make up a plot in nonfiction: if something didn't turn out the way you expected or you would have liked, you're not allowed to write otherwise. Though, of course, you can say that you wish it had turned out otherwise; that's allowable. But as a nonfiction writer, ordering the events into some cause and effect or order of importance is what makes the plot.

THE FAMILY HISTORY STORY P.A.T.H.

The path to any great family history story consists of four elements. I'm going to give you a very simple formula for identifying the plot structure of your family history story.

We are going to call our system The Family History Story P.A.T.H.

Once we have our P.A.T.H., we can begin to expand on it and fill in the details.

P - PROTAGONIST ANCESTOR *Leading character / main figure*

P is for Protagonist Ancestor; every story must tell a story through the viewpoint of a single ancestor. Ancestors are why we dedicated an entire workbook to understanding our most authentic ancestor. Before you can dive into your story P.A.T.H., you must choose one ancestor that will be the focus of your story, the viewpoint through which to tell the family history. You must know this ancestor most

24

wholly, on a very intimate level. Without that knowledge, you cannot understand his goals, his motives for seeking that goal and why it means so much to him. They too are important in your story path.

A - AIM

A is for what your protagonist ancestor is aiming to achieve. Every protagonist has a goal; the same holds for your protagonist ancestor. You must build your plot around a goal they had in their life.

Behind the goal are your ancestor's motivations and the stakes that are at play if they do not achieve this objective. Why does this goal matter to your ancestor in a profound and personal sense? The more it matters to your ancestor the more it will matter to your readers. Every ancestor has a motive for achieving their goal. Outward motives are easy to see, through the outer circumstances of their lives, the context of history going on around them. But it is inner motives that usually drive a person, the personal stakes. It is a lot of work to find those inner motives, but the result will be a much more gripping family history story. Why do we say what we do, get up in the morning, make the decisions and choices that we make in our lives. We feel that what we do matters. No one lives feeling that their life is not without purpose. When life tests us, our motives grow greater. Our deepest convictions rise to the surface. We become determined more than ever, to make a difference, to persist, to not give up and to overcome the odds. By identifying the aim, the goal of your ancestor and the stakes and motivations behind that target, you will also be able to identify your ancestors deepest beliefs, getting inside their head and understanding their inner journey as well as their outer journey.

T – TROUBLE

T is for the troubles your ancestor faced. No goal is achieved without overcoming obstacles, if easily accomplished then it isn't much of a goal. The plot is an account of the many complications thrown in the way of your ancestor as they set out to achieve their ambition. These complications could be internal or external or both. This trouble comes from the antagonist in our stories. Is there an antagonist in your family history? Or is your ancestor her worst enemy? Regardless, it does not matter who complicates your ancestor's life, as long as someone or something does. Without it we have little story to tell. Of course, the bigger the trouble, the better the story.

H - HAPPILY EVER AFTER

H is for Happily Ever After. What did your ancestor accomplish as a result of their struggles and journey? The Happily Ever After is the resolution to your ancestor's story. In nonfiction writing, the promise does not necessarily mean that your ancestor solved their problem, but they have a better understanding it, the world and themselves.

In nonfiction writing, real life doesn't necessarily present you with lovely, tidy endings in which all problems are solved, and, of course, you certainly can't invent a happy ending — or any ending that didn't happen. That's okay. Your resolution just means that the story ends somewhere different from where it started. By the end of your story, your ancestor should have changed, grown or learned something new. This movement is critical to a story. Staying the same is not an option.

Is your ending going to be sad or happy? Sad endings are tricky. It is complex to make a reader sit still and read on when the story in front of him begins to take on the unmistakable gloominess. While it is better to end a story with a satisfying ending for the reader sometimes, those sad endings are inevitable, and it's the call of the writer.

Use the worksheet on the following page to take the path to your family history story.

THE STORY P.A.T.H. WORKSHEET

PROTAGONIST ANCESTOR

Who is the protagonist ancestor of your story?

_____

_____

Why do you believe they are the hero of your story?

_____

_____

What inner journey do you believe your ancestor embarks on through the story?

_____

_____

_____

AIM

What is your ancestor's goal?

_____

_____

_____

Why does this goal matter so much to your ancestor? (motivation)

_____

_____

_____

What is at risk if your ancestor does not achieve his/her goal? (stake)

_____

_____

_____

TROUBLE

What is your ancestor's main conflict?

_____

_____

_____

_____

What are the obstacles that deepen your ancestor's main conflict?

_____

_____

_____

_____

Arrange the obstacles in order of lowest to highest tension?

1._____

2._____

3._____

4._____

5._____

6._____

HAPPILY EVER AFTER

What does your ancestor achieve?

_____

_____

_____

How does your ancestor change from the beginning of his story to the end?

_____

_____

_____

If he does not achieve his goal, what does he settle for?

_____

_____

_____

THE STORY P.A.T.H

Let's write a simple structure plan using our P.A.T.H system.

My Protagonist Ancestor is_____

His/Her aim is to_____

He/She is troubled, and confronted by_____

who opposes his/her because_____

The ending will be when_____

CHAPTER 5

Narrative Structure

"The mark of a master is to select only a few moments but give us a lifetime."

Robert McKee

In creative nonfiction, the structure is the sequence of events and how the writer orders those events to tell the story. The family history writer retells their family history using character, settings, and scenes: added to these elements may be historical facts, theoretical explanations, or a fusion of time and characters. A family history writer must select and arrange these elements depending on a primary purpose, using one of the forms reviewed below.

In the book, Art of Creative Nonfiction, author Lee Gutkind refers to the structure as

"frame is a way of ordering and controlling the writer's narrative so that the story is presented in an orderly and interesting way."

The writer can use any of the following frames:

1. CHRONOLOGICAL STRUCTURE

The chronological structure is the most common use in history writing. However, it can become tiring to tell your ancestor's story in a cradle to grave approach. Instead, consider starting your story from a dramatic point in your ancestor's life, or isolating a particular period in your ancestor's life that holds great adventure. The writer uses the universal story to narrate the story from beginning to end but avoiding a life's chronology of cradle to grave.

2. MANIPULATING STRUCTURE

You can tell your family history story by compressing time, using flashbacks, or flash-forwards or by beginning in the middle of the story. By using a manipulating structure, your story can be far more appealing than a birth to death tale that family historians tend to lean on to tell their stories. Consider showing your account from present to the past, this is a more sophisticated approach as you face linking the chapters and scenes in reverse order, but it can make for a more original structure and read.

3. CIRCULAR STRUCTURE

In this structure, the story ends where it begins. For instance, the writer circles back to the beginning, by repeating a key phrase, or image from the opening of the story at the end of the story giving the reader closure through a full circle approach.

4. PARALLEL STRUCTURE

In this technique, the writer tells two separate stories that converge into a single narrative. This structure conveys two parallel lives that converge, for instance with the marriage of two ancestors.

5. COLLAGE STRUCTURE

The writer constructs a collage by obtaining information from various sources or images. For instance, the author assembles a personal essay from memory, library research or interviews. These assorted parts are combined to form a whole.

6. BRAIDING STRUCTURE

The writer blends two or more stories and merges or intersects them at some point, usually to make a comparison and indicate out some significance.

Which type of structure should you choose to write your family history story? The writer must make his own creative decision. There is no one particular way to determine which story structure to use. Some stories will work well with a particular structure. It will depend on the story and the research you have obtained. You must experiment and rewrite to determine which will work best for your story.

CHAPTER 6

Scene and Summary

"There's always room for a story that can transport people to another place."

J.K. Rowling

Before you can begin to plot your story you first must understand, that stories are a chain of scenes and summaries. The story map that we will learn about in the coming chapter will help you place those scenes and summaries in order that makes sense, creating rising tension and thereby creating suspense for the reader. To do that, you need to understand what constitutes a scene and a summary.

SCENE

A scene is the smallest unit of a story, aside from the sentence. We have the story, and sections and or chapters followed by scenes. Scene and summary are not created equal. First most scenes will show while summaries tell. I'm sure you've heard the mantra, if not from me, then somewhere else, **"show, don't tell."**

In fact, we need to show-and-tell when we write stories. The reason many writing teachers use the mantra of show don't tell is because many writers don't show at all, they merely tell. Not showing is especially true for family history writers. As writers who spend much of their time writing reports, they have a difficult time transitioning to story and using scene and summary to tell their stories. Often when telling a story, they tend to slip back into narrative summary instead of placing the reader in real-time.

It is important to recognize the difference between scene and summary, first, so you can avoid slipping back into dry narrative and secondly, so you can properly arrange your scenes and summary on your family history story map.

In Workbook Number 4,(to be released in 2016) we will roll up our sleeves and examine scene and summary and how to write them. But for now, let's understand what they are so we can arrange them in our outline.

Stories are in fact a structure, a chain of events that take us from our ancestor's desire to achievement. In a scene, we walk in the shoes of our ancestor and feel what he feels. Scenes should happen in real-time. Instead of merely reading the words on the page, we feel a part of our ancestor's world. The reader experiences it as the ancestor experiences it. As the reader gets to know your ancestor with each passing page their bond strengthens. They care about them and become emotionally attached. Scenes should show your ancestor moving closer to their goal in moment by moment action. If a scene does not contribute to this overall purpose, it has no place in your story. A scene will bring conflict and tension to the page through dialogue, facial expressions, gestures and in every detail of the character's response. Scenes should be the most important moments in your plot.

When looking for the scenes to plot they should have the following characteristics.

1. Events in your ancestor's life
2. These events must be part of your ancestor's journey to their goal.
3. They will happen in real-time unless they are a flashback or flashforward scene.
4. They will either demonstrate your ancestor's action or reaction to an event.
5. They will take place in a single location.
6. The scene must have a goal.

SCENE GOAL VERSUS STORY GOAL

As mentioned, a story is a chain linked by scenes. Each scene has a goal, each goal being a step forward in your story. One goal leads to a result that prompts a new objective. If they don't link, if one goal is out of place, there is a break in the chain, and the story will falter.

Your story goal is the dilemma that will take your ancestor the entire story to solve. Perhaps, he wants to immigrate to the new world, or buy land or marry the girl next door. If we break your ancestor's goal down, we will find that the overall target consists of smaller goals. For instance, the ancestor who wished to immigrate to the new world, his first goal, may be to earn the money to buy the ticket. The next goal may be finding transportation to the port of departure. The next goal may be surviving the journey, overcoming sea sickness, and finally passing through the port authorities. You can see how each of these smaller scenes, each with their own hurdles, connect, leading the reader to the outcome.

As you move forward with the rest of this workbook, keep in mind that your scene goals will be different from the story goal. Your character may want one of the following:

1. Something material - an object, a person, etc.

2. Something intangible - admiration, information, etc.

3. Escape from something physical - incarceration, pain, etc

4. Flight from something psychological - worry, suspicion, fear, etc

5. Breaking loose from something emotional - grief, depression, etc.

Methods of achieving these goals will often manifest in one of the following ways (although this list certainly isn't conclusive):

1. Seeking information

2. Hiding information

3. Hiding self

4. Hiding someone else

5. Confronting or attacking someone else or ones self

6. Repairing or destroying physical objects

Sometimes it may take several scenes to reach a scene goal.

QUESTIONS TO ASK ABOUT YOUR SCENE GOALS

Once you've identified your scene's goal, stop and ask yourself the following questions:

1. Does the goal make sense within the overall plot?

2. Is the goal essential to the overall plot?

3. Will the goal's complication/resolution lead to a new goal/conflict/disaster?

BETWEEN THE SCENES - SUMMARY

Scenes are paramount in structuring your family history stories, but equally important are what falls between the scenes and that is a summary. Summary is telling. It offers the reader a condensed narrative of what happens, think of the summary as the voiceover of the narrator in a movie. Summary conveys background information. The information is compacted, summarized. Some of you may be writing a family history that spans over an extended period, or over a large geographic area as your ancestor migrates from place to place. It's not possible to tell every movement and every place they migrated too and certainly not every moment will be important to your story. The role of the summary is to help you transition from one location to another, to skip a period. Instead of every single moment played out in a scene, a summary helps the story move forward quickly through time and space. However, tread carefully, too much summary can distance the reader from the story and can become dry and slow the story down. Family history writers are comfortable in writing reports, as we mentioned earlier, and should be wary of slipping into the long narrative summary.

It is important to find the right balance of scene and summary to keep your story a fascinating tale for the reader.

WHEN TO USE SCENE AND SUMMARY

Again, there are no rules when it comes to deciding how to use scene or summary. As the author, this is your choice, and again you are going to look at your research and the story you intend to tell to help decide the story plot. However, here are a few guidelines to help you recognize those opportunities when you may want to contemplate a scene over a summary.

Is it an important event? – Such as a turning point? Keep scenes to significant events that move the story along and hold a meaningful place in the plotline of your story.

Time – Does the time elapse over weeks or months or is it real time? If the action is happening in real time, write a scene. If the action takes place over weeks or months, use summary.

Do you have enough sensory detail? Do you have enough particulars to bring this event to life? Can you give the reader a visual of the event through your description and detail as if it is playing out in front of them? If so then use a scene.

Do you have dialogue? Can you re-create a conversation based on your research, memories or an interview? Then show a scene.

Do you need to convey background information for the reader to understand the event, or need to communicate a lot of information, then use summary.

Do you intend to reflect on an experience, summarize it?

CHAPTER 7

The When, Why, and How of an Outline

"I wisely started with a map." — J.R.R. Tolkien

Few writers have the ability to write a story without an outline. Never does a writer sit down to start writing and things fall into place in perfect order. While some writers can write this way, they face a pretty messy first draft. Never have I heard of a nonfiction writer or a historical fiction writer who is dealing with an immense amount of facts able to write without an outline. You need a plan for all your facts and details about your ancestor's story to fall into place. Nonfiction narrative relies closely on the structure of your story, arranging those facts just right to create a fascinating journey for your reader. Outlining is your ultimate plan, your GPS, your guide to that mesmerizing finished story.

Outlining is different for every writer, and it may take some time for you to figure out what your optimal outline method may be. It can be anything from lists of scenes written on index cards taped to a wall, a circle, a target, or a traditional narrative arc scratched out on a napkin. It may be anyone of these or a combination. Your outline may be a scribbled out list of the five big things you want to include in the piece or twenty random ideas you jotted down in no particular order. I use a combination of mind mapping, a traditional narrative arc and scene index cards to outline a first draft that I will share with you in this workbook. Whichever you choose will all depend on how you think, how much you trust your memory and how your brain best organizes material. I'm a visual person; I rely heavily on visual cues to help me organize my thoughts and stories. The options I'm offering you are very visual in nature. Play with the options; find the one that works for you.

Outlines have several benefits. An outline will help you maintain a focus on your story. An outline will help your memory. It will remind you of all those fascinating things you have in your research that you organized and wanted to include in your story. Outlines are meant to be modified, turned upside down, expanded and contracted and sometimes even abandoned. The outline is a means to the end, it is your structure, your family history plot, your plan, your story map.

An outline will help you during the revision process, especially if you feel your story has gone astray. It will serve as your GPS to get you back on trap. Outlining helps you spot story problems; it gives you that broader big picture view of your story where you see problems earlier before you've written 50,000 words. The outline will also help you put your story in order with a beginning, middle, and end. By outlining you can strategically place information about your ancestors in your story as you go, foreshadowing future events. If you know where you are going in the story, future mysteries can be alluded to and hidden earlier in your plot to provide an added layer of enjoyment and entertainment to your reader. Your outlines can be lists of things you know you want to include in the piece. It offers you an opportunity to see where you can add transitions, where you can fill in the background and historical context or interject facts into a scene or summary.

Outlining is a simple technique, it is about thinking your story out before you write, and some would even say it is writing. I believe the outline begins from the first brain dump or brainstorm of your story until the end of the first draft. Outlining is devising a plan, a map for your story, steps to get from A to Z. It allows us to think deeper about our story before we sit down to write. The shorter the piece you are writing the less your need for an outline. It's possible to hold all the information you need for a piece of writing in your head, maybe. But an outline is also a way to take control of the time. If you are producing a longer essay or book-length piece of work, you can't possibly hold all the information in your mind. When writing family history stories, I can't see how one writes without an outline. We are dealing with far too much information; it is just impossible to keep track of it all, do yourself a favour and outline.

BRAIN DUMPING

Brain dumping is a simple process to get your ideas down about your story ahead of time. It helps you get clearer about what story you want to write. In my brain dump, I include all ideas I have about my story from the ancestor to the events around that ancestor, relationships, conflicts, and complications. I like to use brain dumping in the very early stages of my story. Earlier in this workbook, we discussed the various ways to find stories in your family history. I like to take an ancestor I feel particularly drawn to or one that I have done an Authentic Ancestor Profile on, and I begin to brain-dump my thoughts on that ancestor keeping in mind the ingredients of a good story. What are some story conflicts in the story, obstacles in the ancestor's life, accomplishments? Look at my brain dump diagram below and consider using what you know about your ancestor, from the Authentic Ancestor Profile you completed in workbook 2 and with your research in hand create a brain dump.

Adam Kowalski Story

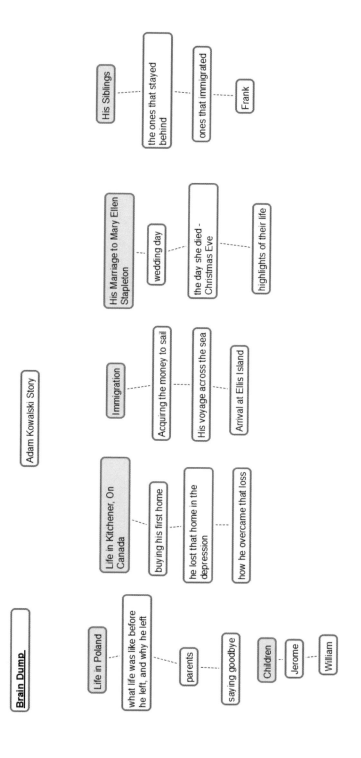

Life in Poland
- what life was like before he left, and why he left
- parents
- saying goodbye

Children
- Jerome
- William

Life in Kitchener, On Canada
- buying his first home
- he lost that home in the depression
- how he overcame that loss

Immigration
- Acquirng the money to sail
- His voyage across the sea
- Arrival at Ellis Island

His Marriage to Mary Ellen Stapleton
- wedding day
- the day she died - Christmas Eve
- highlights of their life

His Siblings
- the ones that stayed behind
- ones that immigrated
- Frank

CREATING A STORY MAP

Once I've done my brain dump, I begin to organize my ancestor's story around the <u>universal</u> story structure. The classic narrative arc follows a straight line, passing through the various plot points of the resolution. This is the start of my story map. Do not feel you have to know precisely, the beginning, middle, and end when you create your story map. When I begin to use a story map, I may have no idea of where the beginning is, or the climax or the inciting incident. I use the story map to help me find these elements, to plot them sometimes multiple times until I find the perfect structure that will tell my ancestor's story in a compelling manner. The Story Map is not a timeline. You are not plotting your ancestor's life on the story map. You are plotting the story. Don't confuse the two. We covered timelines back in Workbook Number 1 - Getting Ready to Write. It is an important tool in organizing your ancestor's life and your research. However, timelines are not your storyline.

Once I've identified the major points on my story map, along with the layers of my map, (these we will cover in the coming chapters), I begin to create a list of scenes and summaries for my story.

CREATING YOUR FAMILY HISTORY
STORY MAP

Our Family History Story Map is a visual guide that represents the universal story.

It allows you to see the dramatic action of your story by seeing how all the scenes work together against the backdrop of the entire piece. It also enables you to track the deeper meaning of your story by adding layers and helps you see the flow of the scenes as they fit together to form your story. The story map allows you to compare your scenes; it permits you to ensure the increase in tension and suspense, heightening the conflict with the flow of the story. The Family History Story Map allows you to to see the big picture, to step back and see your story as a whole and to determine the causality between scenes, the coherence, and flow of the story. It is a visual aid to keep you on track, focused and adhered to a structure.

There several tools that can be used to create a family history story map. If you have a giant whiteboard, you can draw a story map on it. If you happen to have a large chalkboard, they also make a great canvas for a story map. If you have a spare wall in your office, consider painting one with chalkboard paint and create a giant canvas for your family history story map. However, if you don't want to go that far or invest too much money then consider a roll of kraft paper. You can purchase these at your local office supply store. Cut off a 5 or 6-foot strip of paper and draw the story map on your kraft paper.

The map should resemble the mountain on the front cover of your workbook. The story map starts at the bottom left-hand corner and travels upward to a peak about three-quarters of the way across the paper. It then quickly descends into a valley. The line represents the flow of the universal story and is the perfect place to plan your family history story.

Above the lines, you will place the scenes that represent dramatic action, below the line you will place the scenes that are passive, summary and back story or heavy with information.

Get your map ready, as we move through the workbook, we will dig into the three parts of a story, their elements and begin to find them in your story and map them on your story map.

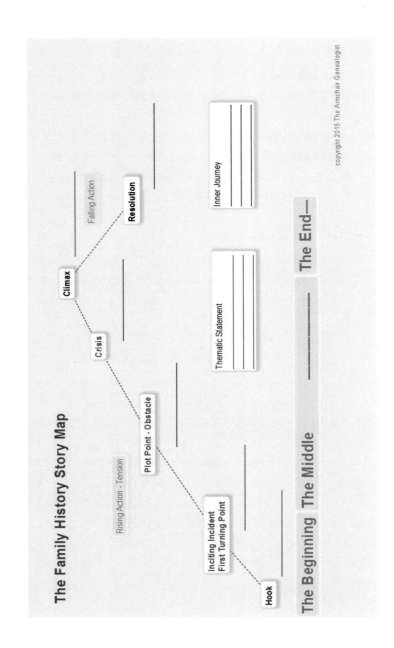

SCENE OR SUMMARY STORY GUIDE (SOS GUIDE)

As I mentioned, once, I have the story mapped, I begin to create a list of scenes and summary. I use two tools for this part of my outline. I use the S0S Guide and index cards. You can use one or the other or both; it is entirely up to you. Play with them, see what works for you.

The SOS Guide allows me to expand on my scene ideas, noting various elements about them. It keeps my scenes in one convenient location so when I'm ready to begin writing these scenes I have an organized overview to keep me focused. I also keep track of summaries on this sheet as well. I can easily see when I need a summary to transition to a new scene and when I need to add backstory or set up a scene. This guide will help you be very purposeful in your thought process and arrangement of your scenes and summary. You'll find an example of the Scene or Summary Story Guide on the following page.

The SOS Guide consists of seven elements that we will consider when writing our scenes.

1. THE SETTING/DATE

Every scene requires us to deal with the time and setting. Sometimes this may be understood from the scenes or summaries that precede it. We are answering the when and where for the readers.

2. THE OUTER JOURNEY

The moment by moment action on the page as the event plays out.

3. THE SCENE GOAL

Your ancestor hopes to accomplish an explicit goal within the scene. Every scene where the ancestor's goal is understood creates a question for the reader to whether they will be successful.

4. TENSION/SUSPENSE

Within the scene is conflict, tension and or suspense. There must be conflict in some form; it does not have to be big and overt, but it does have to be present.

5. INNER JOURNEY

How is the protagonist ancestor emotionally affected by the outer journey? What emotional change happens for your ancestor. This may not necessarily be evident in every scene.

7. THEME

The key to theme lies in your reason for writing the story and what you want your readers to take away from it. Do the details you use in the scene support the theme you have created. Again, not necessary in every scene.

Scene or Summary Guide
SOS Guide

Story Name_____

Scene/ Summary	Setting Date	Outer Journey	Scene Goal	Tension	Inner Journey	Theme
Scene One						
Scene Two						
Scene Three						
Scene Four						

Chapter_____

THE OLD SCHOOL TOOL - INDEX CARDS

Some would say index cards are old-fashioned, but don't discount them; they work. If you are both a tactile and visual person, they will work well for you. Get yourself a package of index cards, I suggest 4 x 6 or 5 x 8 size, so you have enough room to write on them. I recommend picking up two or three colours and I will tell you why shortly. Some people use Post-it notes, I don't mind them for use on a whiteboard for your primary scenes, but I wouldn't use them for a storyboard grid that we are going to create with the index cards. They are just too small to capture all your SOS Guide information on them. Index cards are just more durable than post-it notes.

Each index cards contains a scene or a summary. You can shuffle and reshuffle them until you have them in the right order, in a structure that works, that tells your story. You can pin these to a cork-board, or you can use a tri-fold board, you know the kind that kids use for science projects. They are a good size, and they come folded in exactly the three acts we will be learning about later in this work-book.

Write "Beginning" on the top of the first column, "Middle" at the top of the second column, and "End" at the top of the third column.

1. Write a card saying Hook and pin it to the top of the first column under beginning.
2. Write a card with an "Inciting Incident" and pin it to the bottom of the first column.
3. Write a card say crisis pin it to the bottom of the middle.
4. Write a card saying climax pin it at the top of the third column.

As you work through the next few chapters and worksheets, you can start by filling in these cards with their details. You can begin by just brainstorming the scenes you know will be a part of your story even if you don't know what order they will go in yet. As you sort the order, you can pin them in the appropriate location on either your story map or your storyboard. Every scene and summary go on one card. Of course, this is convenient because you can move them around quite effortlessly. Maybe several cards need to be pinned together to make one scene, or some cards discarded because they don't work. If you think you've got it all figured out on your first go around, you would be wrong.

Some writers will use the index card system before creating a story map or instead of a story map. You can use index cards as your brainstorming tool. Start by jotting down random scenes on index cards as they come to you Organize the cards in an arrangement that follows a narrative arc. For those of you who do not require a visual of the arc, index cards may be a better choice for you. Once you have your scenes, you can use the second colour index card to identify summaries. Again a perfect visual tool for you to see the overall picture and make sure your story is not a lot of summaries but a good balance of scene and summary.

You can use the index card grid instead of your story map or not at all and plot your index cards on your story map. Play around with it until you find the system that works for you.

Here is how I use index cards. I draw a story map on a whiteboard. As I begin to sort my major scenes, I mark them on the whiteboard and create an index card for them pinning them on my story-board. Once I have my key points organized, the beginning, middle, and end, the inciting incident, the crisis, the climax, and resolution, I begin to expand on these by putting them on index cards. I begin to expand on them as well as other scenes and summaries on my storyboard. I choose a different colour index card for summaries. I arrange them in their columns according to the beginning, middle and end. You can also add a third colour if you like to identify your pivotal scenes, the inciting incident, crisis, and climax.

WHAT TO PUT ON THE INDEX CARD

As you begin to expand your story map and the scenes that will take place in the beginning, middle, and end you can write a simple sentence for each scene on an index card. This simple sentence represents the dramatic action or the outer journey of your ancestor. I also leave a place on the card to come back and expand this scene further, perhaps including how the inner journey will show itself in this scene or the theme, the setting, etc. We will cover these in detail in the three parts of a story. Many headings you will see on the SOS Guide you can replicate on the index card. You'll find an example of a scene and summary index card on next page.

Another place to plan your story using index cards is using the index cards contained within the Scrivener writing program. You can replicate the index card system of your story map within Scrivener. It is a simple process; you can easily move index cards and re-order them as you begin to figure our your story structure.

There are plenty of options available for tools and outlining and planning your story. Use the ones I've offered you here, others you may discover or create your own, but please do use a plan to keep yourself on track and focused.

Scene/Summary

Setting/Date:

Outer Journey/Dramatic Action:

Goal:

Inner Journey:

Conflict:

Theme Details:

CHAPTER 8

Layers of Story

"When we want mood experiences, we go to concerts or museums. When we want meaningful emotional experience, we go to the storyteller."
Robert McKee

While your plot line moves in a forward manner, it also has layers. There are three layers to your storyline. They include the dramatic action, the emotional journey of the protagonist and the thematic significance of the story.

The first layer is the dramatic action that is the main physical action and the primary line of on our story map. It represents the physical battle your ancestor moves through on his journey to his goal. We are going to call this the outer journey.

The second layer is the emotional change that occurs in your ancestor as a result of the outer journey. It is represented on our story map and the SOS Guide as the inner journey.

The third layer is the theme, the meaning behind your story.

We've explored the outer journey in detail through the Family History Story P.A.T.H and the Universal Story. While we have mentioned theme and the inner journey briefly, let's spend some time grasping a better understanding before we begin to look for it in our stories.

LAYER 2: THE INNER JOURNEY

Even our most favourite ancestors are flawed. They are ordinary people who are thrust into extraordinary circumstances that are out of their control. After overcoming obstacle after obstacle, they somehow rise above what life has handed them, and they will never be the same again. Our ancestors are changed people once we're done reading their story; they have gone through a transformation, and that change comes with a loss of something that it is dear to them. This is your ancestor's inner journey and the second layer of your family history story.

The inner journey refers to the growth and changes that the reader is going to observe in your ancestor during the story. Demonstrating this growth and change weaved into the dramatic action helps you bridge the divide between your reader and his ancestor. When the reader feels intimately involved with the ancestor, they will feel emotionally connected to that ancestor and thus the story. If the reader is just observing an ancestor going through physical motions but not understanding the effects that those actions have on the ancestor regarding their inner growth and change then the story is empty.

Many family historians struggle with the inner journey, that emotional layer of a story and with good reason. Much of that reason has to do with being researchers and our path being rooted in facts. How can we talk about our ancestor's feelings without a diary that allows us to get inside their head? It's clear if there is an ancestor you have met, interviewed, or you have access to a relative who knew that ancestor, then you acquire some inside knowledge about what they were thinking during the pivotal events in their life. However, for those ancestors, those early ancestors, you never met, it can be a tough task to understand their inner thoughts, but not impossible.

Characterization is our best option for understanding our ancestors. The Authentic Ancestor workbook is crucial in getting to know these ancestors. It will help you to do the research necessary to get inside your ancestor's head. It will show you where to look for those clues to understand your ancestor's thoughts and feelings. We need to see their inner struggles with the conflict and complications they faced and eventually the actions they took to overcome these problems. Emotionally, how do they change when they meet their challenges? I'm not about to reiterate here our lessons on this from Authentic Ancestors; I hope you've done your homework but if not go back and complete your Authentic Ancestor profile to have a personal understanding of your ancestor.

I will mention a few things you should realize can help you to get inside your ancestor's head. Actions, actions, actions are our best clues to how they thought or changed their thoughts about a situation. You know the saying, "*actions speak louder than words*," well this is very true. If your ancestor did one thing and then did an 180-degree turn or even a complete 360, it is not hard to surmise their thoughts and attitudes about a situation changed. For example a young man who signs up for the army only to go AWOL some months or years later, most likely he has gone through an emotional growth and change in his beliefs about war and serving. The challenges he has faced out on the battlefield have irreversibly changed him and his feelings about being part of the war. Even if he stays in the war, no doubt, his take on the world is immensely different than before the war. Your documents, the facts that you have obtained about your ancestors may make the change apparent.

There are many sources where you can seek out information that may provide insight into your ancestors feelings. Newspaper articles, court records, pension applications, diaries, letters, photographs, wills and estate papers can all provide insight into a change of thought in your ancestor's emotional perspective.

Consider using a rhetorical question to create an illusion of thought for your readers. This device will allow you to provide for your reader a possible thought your ancestor may have being feeling without actually stating that you know this for a fact. Worded correctly, it gives your readers insights into possible emotions your ancestor was feeling without crossing the boundaries of nonfiction.

For Example:

Great-Grandpa has sailed to the new world; you may want to impress upon your reader that your great-grandfather may have had some hesitations about whether he was making the right decision. You can use a rhetorical question to present this theory.

As the ship pushed away from the dock, Albert stood at the railing watching the land disappear. Was he wondering whether he had made the right decision?

By using a rhetorical question, I'm not placing a thought in his head that I can't be certain of, but considering whether he may have had that thought.

LAYER 3: THE THEMATIC LAYER

Our family history story is so much more than just the actions our ancestor took, a journey from a to b, the acquisition of something. It reflects a truth. When I say a truth, I don't mean as they relate to the facts. No doubt you are using useful facts. However, a family history story provides a theme, an unwritten philosophical position that your story takes. The individual scenes in your story should add up to this theme. It is not directly stated, or drilled or preached into your reader's head. It lays below the surface and shows itself through symbols, metaphors, and similes.

There are as many themes as there are writers and stories. Just a small sampling to give you an idea.

Loyalty
Responsibility
Abandonment
Good vs. Evil
Love conquers all
Rags to riches
Man vs. Society
Battle
Revenge

Loss of Innocence
Power
Corruption
Sacrifice of self for others

It is quite common not to know what your story is about before you completed your first draft. In fact, I would be surprised if you did. The first draft is often about getting the dramatic action down and understanding the characters. Once you've written that first draft, you've identified all the key points of your story, the beginning, middle and end, the crisis, climax, and resolution, and hopefully after all that the theme will begin to emerge. However, it's important to understand what we mean by theme so we can be vigilant and aware should it present itself. We also want to be able to recognize the premise and make note of it in your theme mind map so that you can produce a thematic statement for your story. It should be something you should always be mindful of as you work on your first draft.

Why does our family history story need a theme? Humans identify with common themes because everyone experiences them somehow. It is another tool for allowing your reader to connect with their ancestor. You have a reason you are writing your family history stories. You have a reason you are writing even this one particular story, beyond just the fact that you want to leave a legacy to your descendants. Look at each story you write and what it means to you, what do you take away from it. It's important to understand your reasons for writing the story, your passion for that story; your voice is how you will express that enthusiasm.

Again we are presented with the idea that we need to find the theme that lays within the dramatic action of our ancestor's story. Finding ideas, turning those ideas into concepts, understanding our ancestor's journey and building in themes and finding your voice are all an important part of finding the story. Writing a story challenges you to figure out what matters most to you about a particular story. Explore and develop the broader meaning and message your story conveys about life, society and ultimately about humanity.

Many family historians shy away from divulging a theme in their story, once again sticking only to the outer journey. However, theme is found by taking the time to step back and analyze what the story may mean to you. Then using your SOS Guide to layer the theme within your scenes throughout the story, with the use of mood, symbols, metaphors, analogies and descriptions.

I'm going to give you a tool to help record your theme ideas that you stumble over as you write your first draft. This tool will help you track those ideas but also draw possible connections between them and ultimately help you create a thematic statement that will sum up your story theme in a clear and concise statement. The Theme Brainstorming Chart will help you stay focused on your theme as you work through future drafts. Finding the theme requires patience. Certainly, some of you who grasp theme already may have a pretty good idea of your theme ideas; you can certainly still plot them on our thematic story map to help you devise your thematic statement.

CREATING A THEMATIC STORY MAP

At the beginning of creating, plotting and outlining your story, theme ideas may emerge from your story that are illustrating the outer journey. The theme of a story can be summed up in a statement demonstrating the meaning behind the story. Once you've obtained your thematic statement, it can be plotted out scene by scene just as the outer and inner journey is plotted.

Let's create a mind map much like we did earlier in the workbook for doing a brain dump of our story ideas. Draw a large oval on a piece of paper or I like to use Scapple for all my mind mapping exercises. Create small ovals that radiate from the larger oval. Fill in the smaller bubbles with themes in your story. You may find yourself thinking about things like, greed, injustice, rebellion, and connect the circles that are similar or compliment each other.

The more you delve into them, the more you'll notice themes all around you. If new topics pop up, add more bubbles. Like any mind mapping exercise, you can use a piece of paper, index cards or Post-it notes. It's not important which tool you use, only that you learn to use mind mapping to record your thoughts about theme on your quest to developing a thematic story statement.

BRAINSTORMING A THEME

Begin with the smaller bubbles. As you write your draft, jot down theme ideas that you see in your story into these small bubbles. As new themes crop up place them in new bubbles. If some of your theme ideas are somehow relevant to each other, connect them with lines. If you are using index cards or Post-it notes, line them up in columns if you find them to be related.

Your goal is to create a statement in the center oval that best represents the major themes from the bubbles. There are as many themes and statement as there are writers and stories. There is no correct answer. The thematic statement will be what you pull from the story, what it means to you and the message you want it to convey to your reader.

You can also work backward. If you already have what you believe is the thematic statement of your story, insert it into the middle and as you work through your first draft, fill the smaller bubbles with examples of that theme in your draft.

Now that you know the theme of your story, you want the details, description, metaphors to reflect the thematic significance of the overall story. Mark on your story map where you find these scenes with objects and metaphors or descriptions that reinforce the overall theme you've created for the story. Record your thematic statement on your story map.

In the next three chapters, we will move through the three parts of a story. In each part, we will address the three layers of the story with the various story elements contained within each section. At the end of each chapter, there are questions in the worksheets that specifically will help you address these story elements and the three layers in writing your family history story.

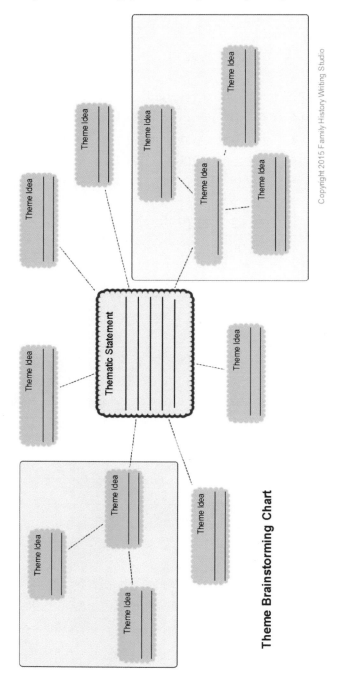

Theme Brainstorming Chart

CHAPTER 9

The Beginning

It's now time to think way back to your high school English class. Remember those brutal days of reading Shakespeare. I bet you thought you would never use that again. Well, this is it, that time has come. If you recall Shakespeare's plays, they were delivered in three acts. In fact, writers have been writing stories in three acts since Aristotle. This structure remains steadfast in story writing and, therefore, holds for writing your family history stories today.

The key to the three act story is arranging a sequence of events that will keep the reader turning the pages. Instead of telling a family history narrative that says this happened, then this happened then that happened. The events rise in action and suspense through three very distinct story parts.

Today we call these three acts the beginning, middle, and end and each part serves a purpose to the larger story and to setting up the story for the next part.

We're now ready to look at each part, their purpose, and some exercises to help you plot your story with a beginning, middle, and end.

THE OVERALL PURPOSE

The beginning is the first quarter of the entire story. Part one is all about introductions and intrigue, and it's also about setting the stakes for you hero's ultimate quest. In the beginning, the principal objective is to make the reader care about your story and more specifically care about your protagonist ancestor. In Part 1, you will introduce us to your ancestor and make it impossible for us not to fall in love with him. We will want to root for him. Part 1 will include a hook, an event that will grab your reader's attention, it will include world-building scenes that will reveal your ancestor in their everyday world. The beginning will introduce the reader to when and where the story takes place. In the beginning, your ancestor will face a conflict, dissatisfaction, restlessness in his everyday world. Tension grows, and he must separate himself from his current existence to begin a journey toward an unknown world. By the end of the beginning, we, the reader, should have an understanding of a goal your ancestor is seeking and what is at stake if they do not reach that goal. We will also understand what are the possible consequences if the protagonist ancestor does not choose a new path.

CHECKLIST - THE BEGINNING

- ■ Get the reader hooked to their family history story
- ■ Create an emotional bond between the protagonist ancestor and the reader.
- ■ Introduce other major characters
- ■ Establish the overall tone, mood, and setting of your ancestor's world
- ■ Introduce the conflict to your ancestor's goal
- ■ Compel the reader to care and to move on to the middle of the story

HOW DO WE GET OUR READERS HOOKED?

A hook is an event that happens early on to "hook" as it implies your reader into the story. Hooks are usually exciting and fun scenes but don't have to offer context to the story or meaning to the reader. They are a tool to draw the reader in while buying you time while you set up the story and introduce the reader to your protagonist ancestor and their world. The hook must be something interesting otherwise it has not done its job. It needs to be something that grabs the reader emotionally, is experienced sensually and makes the reader react. The hook promises something, creates a question that will be answered later as a payoff for reading.

Your opening image should include four elements. First, it gives us the name of your protagonist ancestor and puts that ancestor into action, whether it is in dialogue or he is doing something, but put him in motion immediately. We talked about how your family history story needs to consist of scene and summary, consider opening with scene filled dramatic action. In those opening lines, we also need to get a feeling that something is about to shake up the ancestor's normal life. If we don't why would we keep reading. No one wants to read about someone's regular life; we want to learn about how they overcame a confrontation in their ordinary life.

CREATE AN EMOTIONAL BOND BETWEEN READER AND ANCESTOR

The biggest obstacle you will face is to demonstrate to your reader that your ancestor is not just a name on a document but a real person with feelings and allowing the reader to see and feel those feelings. Who your ancestor is at the beginning of the story is not the same at the end. The inner journey begins at the start and coincides with the outer journey. As the action progresses through the story, this directly reflects on the ancestor's emotional development. Therefore, your ancestor's traits should be made known at the beginning. Introduce the character and illustrate just what his life was like before facing the problem he wants to overcome. Show the reader how he is trying to make it in the world and show the ordinary world of the ancestor. Show us relationships, his character, what is his appeal. Give us a window into his family, fortune, and friends. Make us like him. Illustrate some surface stuff, appearance, dialogue, dialect, mannerisms, movements, actions and a few under the surface traits, let us see his fears and flaws. Don't make him perfect. Don't just show us good qualities about your protagonist ancestor. Along with those good qualities that make him so likable, we also must have an understanding of his weaknesses. What does your ancestor do that will make him most like the reader. The more your reader identifies with your ancestor, the greater the bond.

WORLD-OVERALL TONE, MOOD, AND SETTING

Present your ancestor's world to the reader. Those first lines, the opening images must give us astonishing description. Make your ancestor's world come to life on the page for your reader. We want to see, hear, smell, taste and feel their world. Allow your reader to experience being a part of that world. Present the ancestor's world to the reader, but not just the setting but what life is like for the ancestor. World-building description will also help to set the tone and mood of the story.

INTRODUCE THE CONFLICT TO YOUR ANCESTOR'S GOAL

By the end of the beginning, your reader needs a good understanding of your ancestor's goal. What is his aim? We've discussed at great length the ancestor's goal in previous chapters. Give it to us in part one so we can begin to wonder how your ancestor is going to achieve this aspiration. The target becomes your story question, the question that will keep your reader reading. He'll want to learn how your ancestor reaches their goal. With that purpose, comes the conflict, the thing that is impeding your ancestor and their objective. Remember the conflict may be an outer conflict, or an inner conflict or both.

To compel the reader to continue reading, you not only have to introduce them to the goal and what obstructs your ancestor, but you must also deliver the stakes. What will happen to your hero if they do not accept the challenge of their quest? What motivates your ancestor? What will happen to your ancestor if they fail at achieving their mission? Understand what is at stake is key to the reader moving on to the middle. The higher the stakes, the more at risk, the more compelling the story.

INCITING INCIDENT

The ending of the beginning includes the inciting incident or the first plot point. Your ancestor has come to an event, a decision that they can't escape or avoid. The event may be planned, a complete accident, or out of their control, but regardless it upsets the balance of their everyday life. This first plot point thrusts your ancestor into a new world, one where everything changes, there is no going back. Your reader is now intrigued, and they will want to discover what will happen to their hero.

Prologues

Be careful in adding a prologue to your story. A writing teacher once told me that prologues are often frowned upon. They tend to be used to dump a lot of information on the reader before the start of the story which of course, is a real turn off for your reader. This can be especially dangerous for a family history writer. Remember, this is exactly what your reader fears, an information dump. They are looking for a story make sure the prologue does the same thing as your first lines, seduce the reader to turn the page. The only thing that is not required in a prologue is to introduce your ancestor, but the same elements should be present, a hook, description, a teaser all with the same goal,

BACKSTORY

It is best to avoid any backstory at the beginning of your tale. Sure you may wish to drop a few bits here and there, but don't go into any long-winded summaries or flashbacks. The backstory belongs in the middle if you need one at all. Backstory will not engage your readers immediately because it is not telling the immediate narrative. We do not need to hear the history straight away. It can be more valuable to withhold the backstory, do your best to deny it as long as possible. It can aid with the suspense of your story. Few writers can deliver backstory in the beginning, try to steer clear of it. By holding off and keeping your ancestor's history vague and making the reader wait, you allow the reader to participate in the story and fill in the blanks. In fact, Martha Alderson, The Plot Whisperer suggests you do your best to write your first draft without the backstory. Only then will you accurately know if it is necessary.

THEME

You are well versed in theme by now. The theme of your family history is what your story is truly about. In the beginning, themes are represented through symbols, metaphors, and similies, mood, and setting. If you are just beginning your story, stay watchful for themes that arise in the scenes you write. Use your Theme Chart to help you keep track of your ideas.

SECONDARY CHARACTERS

Of course, your ancestor most likely will not be alone in this story, and there will be other characters that you will need to introduce both in the beginning and in the middle. In the beginning make sure these secondary characters remain just that secondary. Don't spend a lot of time on them, keep your focus on your protagonist ancestor, don't distract your reader by long tangents about an ancestor's parents or spouse. If that information is relevant to the story save if for the middle where you can use it more strategically to reveal something about your ancestor.

On the following pages, after each part of the story you will find worksheets to help you dissect your story and come to understand the three layers of the outer journey, inner journey, and theme. Don't be alarmed if you cannot answer all the questions on the first couple of passes. It will take several attempts at understanding and mapping your story before you will be able to fill in all the questions and have a clear understanding of your story.

The Beginning Checklist

Complete the Beginning Checklist to help you understand the beginning of your story and the information to be conveyed in the opening scenes.

SETTING

Describe the setting of your ancestor's world in the beginning of your story.

_____

_____

_____

What does the setting represent about your ancestor?

_____

_____

_____

How does the setting convey your ancestor's difficulties and circumstances?

_____

_____

_____

What mood will this setting instill in the reader?

_____

_____

_____

_____

How does the mood at the beginning contrast with and or foreshadow the setting and mood coming later in the story?

_____

_____

_____

_____

What main action takes place at this setting?

_____

_____

_____

OUTER JOURNEY

What is your ancestor's goal upon entering the story?

_____

_____

_____

What stands in the way of your ancestor achieving his goal upon entering the beginning of the story.

(Conflict)

_____

_____

_____

What is at risk for your ancestor? What does he stand to lose if he doesn't take this action, or if he takes

the action and fails.(Stakes)

_____

_____

_____

What thoughts preoccupy your protagonist's mind at the beginning of the story?

_____

_____

_____

What does the protagonist believe about life that affects what he/she wants know at the beginning of the

story?

_____

_____

YOUR HOOK

Describe your opening hook. What event do you plan to use to draw your reader in.(the beginning of the beginning)

_____

_____

_____

_____

INCITING INCIDENT

What is the action that your ancestor takes that catapults him into his new world. The point of no return. (end of the beginning)

_____

_____

_____

_____

_____

_____

What does your ancestor leave behind?

_____

_____

_____

What is interfering with your ancestor moving into the middle of the story? (antagonist)

_____

_____

_____

What enables your ancestor to move into the middle?

_____

_____

_____

THEME

List the themes introduced at the beginning of your story. (leave this blank if you are not sure yet or feel free to include some speculations on your part)

_____

_____

_____

_____

Compile a list symbols, metaphors and similes you could use to convey the themes listed previously.

_____

_____

_____

_____

INNER JOURNEY

What is your ancestor's flaw or greatest fault?

_____

_____

_____

What is your ancestor's greatest strength?

_____

_____

_____

What does your ancestor hate?

_____

_____

_____

What is your ancestor's greatest fear?

_____

_____

_____

What is your ancestor's dream?

_____

_____

_____

What is your ancestor's secret? (If applicable)

_____

_____

_____

What traits of your ancestor directly impact the course of the action in the story and are introduced at the beginning.

_____

_____

_____

How do your ancestor's fears, flaws, prejudices, and strengths at the start of the story contrast with her fears, flaws, prejudices, and strengths at the end of the story? (Leave blank if you are not sure yet)

_____

_____

_____

Which of the necessary skills, knowledge, and abilities does your ancestor need for success at the climax and that are missing at the beginning?

_____

_____

_____

_____

What flaws or fears in the beginning foreshadow and contribute to the crisis in the middle?

_____

_____

_____

_____

Why will your readers care about your ancestor in the beginning?

_____

_____

MAP THE BEGINNING SCENES ON YOUR
STORY MAP

Now turn to your story map and place your key scenes on the map. These will include the hook and the inciting incident.

STORY SCENE GUIDE

Use your SOS Guide to track the events that take place at the beginning of your story. Be sure to include not only the outer journey/dramatic action, but the inner journey of the ancestor and any themes. You can jot these topics down on your Theme Brainstorm map. Identifying them will help you deepen and expand every scene.

INDEX CARD STORYBOARD

Create an index card for your hook and inciting incident and write what you believe will represent these scenes. On your storyboard, on the first third of the map under 'beginning' pin the hook. On the bottom of the beginning column pin the inciting incident. Include any other scenes or summaries from the beginning of your story that will take place between these two major points in your story.

Scene or Summary Guide
(SOS Guide)

Story Name_____

Chapter_____

Scene/ Summary	Setting Date	Outer Journey	Scene Goal	Tension	Inner Journey	Theme
Scene One						
Scene Two						
Scene Three						
Scene Four						

Notes:

CHAPTER 10

The Middle

OVERALL PURPOSE

In the middle of the story, the protagonist ancestor works toward achieving her desire. However, with this comes uncertainty. The purpose in the heart of your story is to share this information bit by bit building tension for the reader. It is with suspense that you as a family history writer will keep your reader engaged through the longest section of our story, the middle. Suspense is achieved by dripping your information a little at a time, organizing your events in order of suspense, and ending each chapter leaving us hanging, wondering what is in store next for your ancestor.

THE MIDDLE CHECKLIST
- Response to the inciting incident
- The second plot point
- Response to plot point two
- Other plot points and there responses
- Create suspense and tension
- Bring the ancestor to the crisis moment.

RESPONSE TO THE INCITING INCIDENT

The beginning of the middle begins with your ancestor's reaction to the inciting incident, the event that catapults your ancestor into a new world towards his quest. The centre will comprise of several plot points that will deepen your ancestor's challenge to reach his goal. The middle is the longest part of your story and can often be the toughest area to keep your reader engaged. Divide the middle into two parts to resist the infamous sagging in the middle.

In the first half, the ancestor figures out what to do, wonders, gets ready for the coming conflict or takes a journey of discovery, makes friends and enemies, gets advice, gets into trouble, explores his options, etc. The middle reminds the reader of the conflict, and the powerful force the ancestor is up against. At the midpoint, the middle of the story, this plot point is the game changer. The midpoint kicks off the second half of the middle. The stakes that your ancestor faces will become all too apparent as he moves through the middle of the story. You need to weave this into your ancestor's storyline.

The second half of the middle introduces your ancestor to more complex obstacles. He will work harder, and eventually will face the most difficult obstacle of all, the crisis point.

PLOT POINTS

The middle will comprise of several plot points that will deepen your ancestor's challenge to reach his goal. We've mentioned plot points earlier but let's take a closer look at them. A plot point is an event that changes everything for the character. It creates a new story question, a new quest, and new motivations. These plot points may include barriers or complications on your ancestor's journey. In your story, plot points are the major events. They are turning points. There may be temporary triumphs only to face another barrier, and there may be moments where the goal is pushed farther out from your ancestor. Depending on the length and pacing of the story, you could have many plot points. On some level, every scene offers the potential to be a plot point. Plot points occur whenever something happens that changes your ancestor's perceptive of the conflict and his understanding of how to react to it.

Every story has three major plot points at the 25%, 50%, and 75% mark. The first major plot point occurs at the end of the beginning; we call this the inciting incident. We've already discussed this plot point in the previous chapter, The Beginning. Halfway through the middle, we find the second major plot point, it moves your ancestor so much that they are no longer just reacting to their antagonist, but they start taking deliberate action against the antagonist force. Martha Alderson, the author of The Plot Whisperer, refers to this as the Recommitment Scene. Think of it as your ancestor having a renewed energy to reach his goal. The third plot point occurs at the 75% mark, it will be the lowest point for your ancestor, it is the infamous crisis. Out of this plot point, your ancestor finds a new determination to meet and defeat his antagonist in the climax, the final turning point. In the climax your ancestor faces his opponent one last time, only this time, the outcome will be for the better.

HOW TO BUILD SUSPENSE

1.BIT BY BIT
One technique for building suspense is to reveal your story a little at a time. If you give the reader too

much upfront, they have little reason to keep reading.

2. End with Cliffhangers

Look at the events in your ancestor's research, which lend themselves to becoming cliffhangers. We need to leave the reader wondering what happens next. The best place to create suspense is at the end of chapters or sections. You set yourself up to resolve the question in the next chapter and encourage the reader to keep turning the pages to know the answer. Always end your chapters and scenes with a challenge, obstacle, complication, speculation or a question. Begin each new scene or chapter or section with the reaction to that problem. Ending a scene with a challenge and opening the follow chapter with a response to the change is one way to keep your readers engaged and turning the pages.

3. Stay on Track

Also, make sure you keep your story on focus. Don't take your reader off on tangents that have little to do with the story. All too often I see stories that begin to tell us about some interesting history of the town or details of an event that has no relevance to the ancestor's story. Also, watch out for introducing a new ancestor to the story and going off on a tangent about that ancestor. If you lose your focus in the middle, you most likely have lost your reader. Don't turn your story into a history lesson but stay focused on your ancestor's journey weaving your historical facts into the scenes and summary bit by bit.

BACKSTORY

The middle is the best place to introduce your ancestor's back story. Now back story is just not a place to dump all your research, every detail you know about that ancestor. Your information in the backstory must be relevant to present story. It serves to deepen our understanding of the ancestor. The explanation of what is in the past made the ancestor who he is today. Choose this information wisely.

The best time to reveal the backstory of your ancestor is right before he is about to embrace change in the climax. Events that happened to your ancestor in the past can often shed light on why your ancestor acts the way he does. It shows where the beliefs, fears, and prejudices come from that he has struggled with for so long.

Flashbacks and summary are often the tools of choice to deliver back story. As we discussed in the previous chapter, flashbacks are best used in the middle. Using flashbacks at the beginning before the present story is established will disorient the reader. The other tool for backstory is a narrative summary. Often backstory is told to us through the narrative summary. Be careful when using narrative summary it can quickly turn into a dry long-winded unraveling.

If you get through the middle or even the entire story without the backstory, chances are you didn't need it after all. If you spend a lot of time in the backstory, perhaps that is the story you should be writing.

SECONDARY CHARACTERS

In the middle, there most likely will be other characters who join the story. They present as friends in your ancestor's quest or antagonists that interfere with your ancestor's progress. Don't begin to introduce these secondary characters too soon, not until you've introduced your protagonist ancestor to the reader and they have established a bond with him.

The antagonist controls the middle of the story. The antagonist is an external or internal force that spends most of the middle interfering with your ancestor's progress toward his goal.

CRISIS POINT

At the three-quarter mark of your story, or the end of the middle, your story rises to a breaking point. Each scene in the middle marches your ancestor toward the crisis. The crisis is a plot point, an event that your ancestor must overcome, like all others, however, the crisis should be the plot point that offers the most tension, suspense and ultimately emotional transformation for your ancestor. It will be the lowest point for your ancestor in his quest towards his goal. The crisis rests in the ancestor's storm path. The storm path is that one place that holds power over your ancestor. The crisis point is the antagonist's climax, where your ancestor fails, the antagonist prevails.

Sidebar

If you're writing a legacy family history book and you have a few small stories about people who not part of your main story or a little history about a place and then consider a sidebar. Use a sidebar to insert these stories without distracting from your main story. If will all depend what kind of family history book you're writing a book.

The action at the crisis should reveal more about your ancestor's emotional profile and maturity as he faces his breaking point. The crisis shows the emotions of your ancestor. The crisis jolts the ancestor into a new acceptance, one that begins his transformation. After the crisis, everything changes.

INNER JOURNEY

During the middle, your ancestor deals with his fears. Perhaps he fails in an attempt to be a hero or to face his inner demons. Your ancestor reacts under stress, has help from friends, and battles his emotions. He might worry about something unknown. In the middle, your ancestor also takes inventory of his strengths and weaknesses and reconciles his flaws and demons finally pushing back against the antagonist. He is moving toward personal change, he is still the same person we first met, but the reader might see a slight alteration.

THEME

In the beginning, you took the time to identify a few overall themes for your story. You used symbols, metaphors, and similes to develop these themes in the beginning. You will further develop these ideas into the middle. Some of these themes may drop off in the middle while others will carry forward. As the ideas deepen in the middle, they will foreshadow what will come at the crisis and the climax.

The Middle Checklist

Complete the Middle Checklist to help you identify the information you need in the middle of your story and to help you identify the middle scenes.

SETTING

Describe the setting of the middle of your story.

_____

_____

_____

How does the setting your ancestor just left differ from the setting he enters?

_____

_____

_____

How does the mood and tone in the new world differ from the mood and tone in the old world?

_____

_____

_____

What is the atmosphere of the new setting in the middle of the story?

_____

_____

_____

_____

What sights, sounds, smells, and tastes are found in the new world setting for the middle of the story?

_____

_____

_____

What about the new world setting excites or concerns your ancestor protagonist.

_____

_____

DRAMATIC ACTION

What new goals arise as a reaction to the inciting incident?

_____

_____

_____

How does your ancestor's original goal get pushed further out of his reach?

_____

_____

What main plot point takes place in the middle of the story that forces your ancestor to stop reacting and start acting on the antagonist force?

_____

_____

_____

_____

Why is your protagonist ancestor taking this action?

_____

_____

How does this action contrast with the action in the beginning of the story?

_____

_____

_____

How does this action differ from the action in the end?

_____

What does your protagonist ancestor want now that he is in the middle of the story?

_____

_____

_____

Describe the setting of the crisis?

_____

_____

_____

What does the setting represent for your ancestor? Fear? Change?

_____

_____

_____

THE CRISIS

What happens to your ancestor at the crisis?

_____

_____

_____

_____

List all the reversals of fortune that your ancestor experiences at the crisis.

_____

_____

_____

What beliefs or behaviours are stripped from, lost or killed in your ancestor due to what happens at the crisis?

_____

_____

_____

_____

INNER JOURNEY

How does your ancestor enter the middle of the story? Confused? Fearful? Excited? Sad? Hopeful?

_____

_____

_____

How open is your ancestor to the changes in the setting and themes that now surround him?

_____

_____

Does your ancestor show an engagement or an aversion to the unknown ahead of him now that he is in

the middle of the story?

_____

_____

_____

Who is the ancestor in the middle of the story compared to who he was at the beginning?

_____

_____

_____

Who is the ancestor in the middle of the story compared to who he becomes at the end of the story?

_____

_____

_____

How does the plot point in the middle of the middle help your ancestor to have a clearer understanding

of the conflict and his own reactions to it?

_____

_____

_____

What personal fear, flaw and or prejudice must he become aware of and overcome for his ultimate success at the end of the story?

_____

_____

_____

Is this the same trait that was evident in the beginning?

_____

_____

_____

How does this trait intensify its interference in the middle of the story?

_____

_____

_____

What flaws or fears in the middle foreshadow and contribute to the crisis that is coming later in the middle?

_____

_____

_____

What is your ancestor thinking about?

_____

_____

_____

Where do those thoughts send the energy of the story?

_____

_____

_____

_____

How does what your ancestor believe about life affect what he wants now in the middle of the story?

_____

_____

_____

_____

What about your ancestor intrigues the reader enough to want to continue reading?

_____

_____

_____

_____

What does the action in the crisis reveal about your ancestor's internal makeup and emotional maturity?

_____

_____

_____

Antagonist

List all of the antagonists who control the world in the middle, in order of importance to the storyline.

_____

_____

_____

How does the most important antagonist interfere with your ancestor's journey towards his goal?

_____

_____

_____

How do the antagonists reflect and foreshadow in the middle of the action what is coming at the end?

_____

_____

_____

Which antagonist triggers your ancestor's fear, flaw, and or prejudice? How?

_____

_____

Which of the necessary skills, knowledge, and abilities needed by your ancestor for success at the climax does the antagonist embody?

_____

_____

_____

How are the antagonist's personal traits different from your ancestor's traits?

_____

_____

_____

What does the antagonist do in the middle?

_____

_____

_____

_____

Why is he doing it?

_____

_____

_____

What does the antagonist want?

_____

_____

How do the antagonist's goals directly oppose your ancestor's goals?

_____

_____

THEME

List the themes that are present in the beginning of your story and continue into the middle of the story.

_____

_____

_____

List any new themes that you discover in the middle of the story.

_____

_____

MAP THE MIDDLE SCENES ON YOUR
STORY MAP

Now turn to your story map and place your key scenes on the map. These will include the plot points and the crisis.

SCENE OR SUMMARY GUIDE

Use your SOS Guide to track the events that take place in the middle of your story. Be sure to include not only the outer journey/dramatic action, but the inner journey of the ancestor and any themes. You can jot these ideas down on your Theme Brainstorm Chart. Identifying them will help you deepen and expand every scene.

INDEX CARD STORYBOARD

Create an index card for your plot points and the crisis and pin them to your storyboard in the middle column. Include any other scenes or summaries for the middle of your story.

Scene or Summary Guide
SOS GUIDE

Story Name_____

Chapter: _____

Scene/ Summary	Setting Date	Outer Journey	Scene Goal	Tension	Inner Journey	Theme
Scene One						
Scene Two						
Scene Three						
Scene Four						

Notes:

CHAPTER 11

The End

OVERALL PURPOSE

The overall purpose of part three is to have your reader leave the story satisfied. Your ancestor faces his last obstacle to reaching his goal. It will test his faith, his resolve, his character, both emotionally and physically. The end will offer closure for the reader. It will answer all their questions. However, equally important, we hope the reader will observe a transformation in their ancestor and come away from the story with a message, a teaching they will carry with them, that will inspire them to know more about their family history.

The ending may manifest in a few ways. Your ancestor will get what they want, or they barely survive and escape to fight another day. Regardless, if your ancestor doesn't attain his goal, the reader is satisfied with a compromise. If you plan on writing a collection of short stories, a series of family history books or maybe a blog, you want the reader coming back for more. Therefore, you may want to solve just enough to make the reader happy, but leave a little room for a future story or the next book, blog post, or short story.

CHECKLIST

- The Climax
- Loose ends tied up
- Your Ancestor's Inner Journey and How it Affected Him
- What does the reader learn?
- Closing Image

CLIMAX

The climax is the final event that resolves your story problem. Your ancestor gets validation, victory or a resolution to his goal. Having survived the crisis, your ancestor begins a transformation as he prepares to face his antagonist in the climax. Your ancestor will change and take a new approach as he prepares to come face to face with his enemy one last time. The story question is answered, the problem is resolved, the goal accomplished. In the climax, your ancestor should feel overwhelmed but not your reader. If you have written your story well, they should be ready for the climax. The more opposing the forces or, the greater the magnitude of the forces in opposition the more exciting the climax is for the reader. At the climax, every conviction and instinct your ancestor has is tested. Throughout the story, your ancestor's flaws limit him by whatever injury in his backstory limits his beliefs. As your ancestor moves to the end, the backstory wound is healing, and the climax reveals a healed ancestor.

YOUR ANCESTOR'S CHANGE AND HOW IT EFFECTED HIM

In the resolution, we see the transformation of our ancestor. How is your ancestor different from the beginning of the story. The reader will acquire an awareness of a growth or change in their ancestor from their battle. If the goal is not achieved the ancestor comes to an understanding and acceptance. From this point, the protagonist ancestor responds to what just happened. His attitudes have changed. Life is no longer the same for him.

LOOSE ENDS ARE TIED UP

Loose ends are tied up, and questions get answered. For the reader to feel satisfied at the end of the story, she must be able to assess how the world looks to your ancestor since the change from the beginning. The reader wants to know that your ancestor will proceed with their life using their new found knowledge, and there are no lingering unanswered questions.

CLOSING IMAGE

Your story should end with a closing image that is in direct contrast or reflects the opposite of the opening image in some way. It can almost be a hook to your next story. It can be an actual hook to a sequel, or just a clever way to end that will make the reader want more from you. Such endings offer great promise and a new beginning the reader may never have anticipated as a new story begins. Although the story seems over, the ancestor and her story continue beyond the endings of the page.

The End Checklist

Complete the End Checklist to help you identify the necessary elements that are essential to close out your story.

SETTING

Describe the setting at the end of your story?

_____

_____

_____

What does the end setting represent to your ancestor?

_____

_____

_____

What does the setting at the end of your story convey about your ancestor's choices and circumstances?

_____

_____

_____

_____

What main action takes places at this end setting?

_____

_____

_____

_____

What tone and mood does the end setting instill in the reader?

_____

_____

_____

Describe where the resolution takes place?

_____

_____

_____

DRAMATIC ACTION

How does your ancestor respond to the defeat at the crisis?

_____

_____

_____

Describe your ancestor's action leading up to the climax of the story.

_____

_____

_____

_____

How does your ancestor confront the antagonist in the climax?

_____

_____

_____

What happens to your ancestor during the climax?

_____

_____

_____

_____

Why does your ancestor take these actions at the climax?

_____

_____

_____

What loose ends need to be tied up in the resolution?

_____

_____

_____

_____

How can your ending scene reflect elements of your opening scene?

_____

_____

_____

Does your ancestor's goals propel the story to the ending?

_____

_____

_____

_____

Who or what is your ancestor's greatest foe in the end of the story?

_____

_____

_____

Does the strength and magnitude of the opposing forces at climax build excitement?

_____

_____

_____

_____

INNER JOURNEY

How does your ancestor enter the ending of your story? With hesitation? With confidence?

_____

_____

_____

Which trait of your ancestor is transformed and directly impacts the climax of the story?

_____

_____

_____

What is the greatest self-knowledge that your ancestor gains as he succeeds at the climax?

_____

_____

_____

Who is your ancestor after the climax?

_____

_____

_____

_____

Theme

List the themes that you find present in the end of the story.

_____

_____

_____

List the themes that you are consistent from the beginning of the story to the end of the story?

_____

_____

_____

List any themes that appear at the end of the story that you feel you could now go back and incorporate into the beginning of the story.

_____

_____

_____

List the symbols, metaphors, and similes used to convey the themes in the end.

_____

_____

_____

MAP THE END SCENES ON YOUR STORY MAP

Now turn to your story map and place your key ending scenes on the map. These will include the climax and your closing scene.

SCENE OR SUMMARY GUIDE

Use your SOS Guide to track the events that take place at the end of your story. Be sure to include not only the outer journey/dramatic action, but the inner journey of the ancestor and any themes. You can jot these themes down on your Theme Brainstorm Chart. Identifying them will help you deepen and expand every scene.

INDEX CARD STORYBOARD

Create an index card for your climax and closing scene and pin them to your storyboard on the third column of your board. Include any other scenes or summaries for the end of your story.

Scene or Summary Guide
SOS Story Guide

Name _____

Chapter_____

Scene/ Summary	Setting Date	Outer Journey	Scene Goal	Tension	Inner Journey	Theme
Scene One						
Scene Two						
Scene Three						
Scene Four						

Notes:

Bibliography

Alderson, Martha. The Plot Whisperer. Avon, MA, U.S.A: AdaMedia, 2012.

Carmack, Sharon DeBartolo. You Can Write Your Family History. 1st ed. Cincinnati, OH: Betterway Books, 25 Sept. 2003.

Colletta, John Philip. *Only a Few Bones, A True Account of the Rolling Fork Tragedy and Its Aftermath*. Washington, D.C.: Direct Descent, 2015.

"Family storytelling: Good for children (and parents)." Psychology Today, 5 Mar. 2015.

Feiler, Bruce. "The Family Stories That Bind Us — This Life." *Fashion & Style*The New York Times, 5 Feb. 2015

Franklin, Jon. *Writing For Story*. New York, New York: Penguin Group, Sept. 1994.

Gerard, Philip. *Creative Nonfiction: Researching and Crafting Stories of Real Life*. 1st ed. Cincinnati, OH: Story Press Books, 29 May 1996.

Gutkind, Lee. *The Art of Creative Nonfiction: Writing and Selling the Literature of Reality*. 1st ed. New York: Wiley, John & Sons, 1997.

Hart, Jack. *Story Craft, The Completer Guide to Writing Narrative Non-Fiction*. Chicago, United States of America: The University of Chicago Press, 2011.

Munier, Paula. *Plot Perfect, Building Unforgettable Stories Scene by Scene*. First ed. Blue Ash, Ohio: Writer's Digest Books, 2014.

Palermo, Lynn. *The Family History Writing Studio*. The Family History Writing Studio, 2015.

Palermo, Lynn (Lynn Palermo). "The Armchair Genealogist." 2015,

"Posts about creative nonfiction writing on find your creative muse." 31 July 2013.

Weiland, K.M. *Structuring Your Novel, Essential Keys to Writing Outstanding Stories*. United States of America: Pen for Sword, 2013.

Weiland, K.M. "The Secrets of Story Struture." *Helping Writers Become Authors*. n.d.

Windsor, Steve. *9 Day Novel, Outlining, The Basics*. United States of America: Vixen, 2015.

Yntema, Sharon K, Jill Swenson, and Nikki Kallio. "The importance of narrative arc in non-fiction and memoir." *The Manuscript*. Swenson Book Development, 15 Sept. 201

About the Author

Lynn Palermo

Other Books by Lynn Palermo

The Complete Guide to the Family History Interview
Getting Ready to Write, Workbook 1
Authentic Ancestors, Workbook 2

Lynn Palermo is a genealogy professional with a love for the written word. She conducts classes both in person and through her online classroom The Family History Writing Studio. Lynn instructs family historians on how to find their words through webinars, lectures, eBooks and coaching. The author of her own family history book, *The Waters of My Ancestors*, Lynn knows all too well the challenges genealogists face in writing their narratives and is on a mission to rid the world of the dry family history story. You can also connect with Lynn at The Armchair Genealogist where she offers down-to-earth advice on researching and writing a family history.

The Family History Writing Studio www.familyhistorywritingstudio.com

The Family History Writing Challenge www.familyhistorywritingchallenge.com

The Armchair Genealogist www.thearmchairgenealogist.com

Made in the USA
Columbia, SC
08 March 2018